AMERICAN WOMEN AND POLITICS

GARLAND REFERENCE LIBRARY
OF SOCIAL SCIENCE
(VOL. 174)

AMERICAN WOMEN AND POLITICS
A Selected Bibliography and Resource Guide

Barbara J. Nelson

GARLAND PUBLISHING, INC. • NEW YORK & LONDON
1984

Library of Congress Cataloging in Publication Data

Nelson, Barbara J., 1949–
   American women and politics.

   (Garland reference library of social science ;
v. 174)
   Includes indexes.
   1. Women in politics—United States—Bibliography.
I. Title. II. Series.
Z7964.U49N38 1984 [HQ1236] 016.3054'2   82-49142
ISBN 0-8240-9139-6 (alk. paper)

Cover design by David Kemelman

Printed on acid-free, 250-year-life paper
Manufactured in the United States of America

For
The Students of Women in Politics
at Princeton University

CONTENTS

INTRODUCTION

Scholarship on the subject of American women and politics has increased dramatically in the last decade. The new research has been available not only in books and articles, but also in government publications and the reports of private research organizations. The aim of this volume is to bring together much of this material in one easy-to-use reference work.

Like most bibliographers, I felt enormous enjoyment as the project progressed, enjoyment which stemmed from the knowledge that assembling and organizing existing scholarly research would strengthen the academic infrastructure which encourages future research. Similar efforts to collate material on women and on gender differences are under way all across the academic disciplines. Considered together, these projects have the twin advantages of systemizing research on women and gender for use by specialists, while also making the material available to all scholars who want access to the new research in their disciplines.

Focusing specifically on American women and politics, this bibliography includes over 1,600 citations to books, articles, reports, and public documents, emphasizing work published between 1970 and 1982. The number and diversity of citations signal two important changes—a change in the political activities of women and a concurrent change in the scholarship about women and politics. Many authors included in this book note that women have become more active in the traditionally valued forms of civic expression—voting, campaigning, and seeking electoral office. But the growing volume of research on women and politics does not result solely from examining how women participate in democratic politics. Increased interest also derives from challenging the definition of what is "political." Thus, the bibliography reflects the growing attention given to such non-electoral political concerns as social movements, adult political socialization, and women's role in the welfare state, as well as the renaissance in political theory.

The bibliography is organized in thirteen chapters covering social movements, history, the nature-versus-nurture debate, the family, political socialization, work and leisure, education, democratic political participation, dependent political participation, political leadership, social policy, political theory, and resources for research. Some of these topics are conventionally considered "political" and some are not. Economists claim labor force participation as their bailiwick; sociologists conduct much of the important research on the family; and psychologists discuss the nature-versus-nurture debate. But all of these topics are profoundly political in implication. For instance, it is difficult to understand women's inferior political station without examining the biological "theories" which purport to show that women were (or are) unfit for the rigors of political participation. Moreover, the same biological arguments have been used to keep racial, ethnic, and religious minorities; workers; lesbians; and gay men from full citizenship and active participation. As a consequence of collating the research on the nature-versus-nurture debate as it applies to women, the bibliography marshals some of the resources needed to ask analogous questions for other groups.

Most of the citations listed in the bibliography refer to scholarly books or articles. Every major American publisher (and a host of smaller, more specialized presses) was asked to provide a back list and future publication schedule of books pertinent to women and politics. The article citations were drawn mainly from a review of the *Social Science Index*, the *Humanities Index*, *Women Studies Abstracts*, and the *Public Affairs Information Service* for the years from 1970 through 1982. Citations to articles in popular magazines and newspapers were not routinely included as these materials are easy to locate through the *Readers' Guide to Periodical Literature* and various newspaper indices. There are, however, some exceptions to this rule excluding citations to popular articles. For example, only a small number of scholarly articles and books have been written on the anti-feminist right or by its adherents. To provide more information on this important topic, a number of references from popular media have been included as well.

An enormous volume of material came to light through this search, and it was immediately evident that the bibliography would have to be selective. Three rules were derived to guide the selection process. First, I wanted the bibliography to represent the great diversity of women's experiences. Hence I made a concerted effort to include material on women of every class, race, ethnicity, religion, region, sexual preference, and belief. Second, I wanted to include references to introductory and advanced materials on the same topics. Third, I wanted to include materials that employed a variety of research methods such as the presentation of primary source material, textual analysis, case studies, survey research, in-depth interviewing, demonstration projects, and the like. In the end, however, each decision to include a citation was partly subjective, a necessary response to the explosion of research on women and politics over the last decade.

Certain topics were not emphasized, largely because bibliographic or reference material on them is available elsewhere. I did not highlight the research on violence against women; criminality and gender; abortion, fertility, and contraception; medical care for women; women and religion; women and the media; and women in sports. Readers interested in these topics should check Chapter 13: Reference Resources in Women and Politics for bibliographic citations.

In addition to choosing the citations, the challenge of the project was to make the volume easy to use. To that end the book is divided into thirteen topical chapters, each alphabetized separately. If a citation might sensibly be found in more than one chapter, it is indeed listed in more than one chapter. But the chapters provide only a broad categorization of the citations by topic. For a much finer categorization, readers should employ the subject and author indices.

The book is also organized in a manner which facilitates constructing course syllabi. An examination of syllabi for upper-level Women and Politics courses shows that many teachers begin their courses by discussing social movements and end by discussing social policy; the arrangement of the bibliography reflects this progression. Teachers of introductory and advanced American politics courses can also use the bibliography for materials on women or gender differences.

This book had its origins in teaching. The first, much shorter version of this bibliography was compiled in the summer of 1979, when I returned to teaching after a two-year leave of absence. In the two years I had not taught Women in Politics, the literature had grown enormously. As I reviewed the literature to update my syllabus, I decided to compile the references as well. Two years later, Marie Ellen Larcada of Garland Publishing, Inc., expressed an interest in publishing an expanded version as a reference book. Her support, and later that of Julia Johnson, made the rigors of transforming the bibliography into its present form much less burdensome than they might have been.

In addition to my editors, I am indebted to many people and institutions for their support of this project. My wholehearted thanks go to

Donald E. Stokes, Dean of the Woodrow Wilson School at Princeton University for supporting the project personally and through faculty research resources. Ingrid Reed, Assistant Dean for Administration, was unfailingly helpful in arranging the administrative support crucial to a reference work. Robert Gilpin and Fred Greenstein kindly and consistently alerted me to many citations in their fields of expertise. Ginie Reynolds and Vonnie Vaughn wordprocessed the bibliography with care, professionalism and personal commitment to the endeavor. Marjorie Quick and Bette Keith each ably typed sections of early versions of the bibliography and never lost their patience with the task.

The finishing touches of the bibliography were added while I was a Visiting Fellow at the Russell Sage Foundation. My deeply felt thanks go to Marshall Robinson, Peter de Janosi, Alida Brill, Mariam Chamberlain, Mary Rubin, Sam Cohn, Barbara Farah, and Cynthia Epstein for their encouragement and support. I would also like to thank Leslie Calman and Diane Fowlkes, who commented thoughtfully and perceptively on the manuscript during its last phase.

I would like to acknowledge the special assistance of Bat-Ami Bar On, Wendy Brown, Kirstie McClure, and Amanda Thornton who generously consulted on the political theory chapter as well as offered personal support. They were especially important in deciding which classical texts of political philosophy would be included in the bibliography. On their good advice, this chapter includes citations to political philosophers whose silence (or barely articulated assumptions) about women and gender differences structured the debate over the "woman question" for centuries.

But most of all I would like to thank the research assistants who helped with this project. Carla Hesse, Carol Ryner, Sally Kenney, Norman Foster, and Mandy Carver worked on the project in its final stage and created the indices. Faye Kessin, Kirstie McClure, Lynn Meskill, Kathy Milton, and Amanda Thornton participated in assembling earlier versions of the bibliography. I thank them all for their assistance and enduring friendship.

This book is dedicated with affection and gratitude to the students of Politics 321: Women in Politics at Princeton University.

Barbara J. Nelson
Princeton, New Jersey
July 1983

AMERICAN WOMEN
AND POLITICS

I. A SOCIAL MOVEMENT APPROACH TO FEMINISM AND WOMEN'S RIGHTS

1. Abbott, Sidney and Barbara Love. Sappho Was a Right-on Woman (Briarcliff Manor, NY: Stein and Day Publishers, 1972)

2. Acosta-Belen, Edna and Elia Hidalgo Christensen, eds. The Puerto Rican Woman (New York: Praeger Publishers, 1979)

3. "Ain't I A Woman?" Off Our Backs, Vol. 9 (June 1979)

4. Allen, Walters R. "The Social and Economic Statuses of Black Women in the United States," Phylon, Vol. 42 (March 1981), pp. 26-40

5. Almquist, Elizabeth M. and Mae C. King. "Position Papers: The Status of Black Women: Oppression and Power: the Unique Status of the Black Woman in the American Political System," by Mae C. King: Untangling the Effects of Race and Sex: the Disadvantaged Status of Black Women" by Elizabeth M. Almquist, Social Science Quarterly, Vol. 56 (June 1975), pp. 115-142.

6. Altbach, Edith Hosino, ed. From Feminism to Liberation (Cambridge, MA: Schenkman Publishing Company, Inc., 1980)

7. Altman, Dennis. Homosexual: Oppression and Liberation (New York: Dutton, 1971)

1

8. Amundsen, Kirsten. The Silenced Majority: Women
   and American Democracy (Englewood Cliffs, NJ:
   Prentice-Hall, 1971)

9. Amundsen, Kirsten. A New Look at the Silenced
   Majority: Women and American Democracy (Englewood
   Cliffs, NJ: Prentice-Hall, 1977)

10. Ash, Roberta. "An Analytic Introduction," in her
    Social Movements in America (Chicago: Markham
    Publishing Co., 1972)

11. Ash, Roberta. Social Movements in America
    (Chicago: Markham Publishing Co., 1972)

12. Auerbach, N. "Women On Women's Destiny: Maturity
    As Penance," Masschusetts Review, Vol. 20 (Summer
    1979), pp. 326-334

13. Babcox, Deborah and Madeline Belkin, eds.
    Liberation Now: Writings from the Women's
    Liberation Movement (New York: Dell, 1971)

14. Baer, Judith A. The Chains of Protection: The
    Judicial Response to Women's Labor Legislation
    (Westport, CT: Greenwood Press, 1978)

15. Ball, Margaret E. "Common Factors in Sex and Race
    Discrimination," Psychological Reports, Vol. 44
    (June 1979), pp. 831-834

16. Beck, Evelyn Torton, ed. Nice Jewish Girls: A
    Lesbian Anthology (Watertown, MA: Persephone
    Press, 1982)

17. Becker, Susan D. The Origins of the Equal Rights
    Amendment: American Feminism Between the Wars
    (Westport, CT: Greenwood Press, 1981)

18. Berkin, Carol and Mary Beth Norton. Women of
    America (Boston: Houghton Mifflin, 1979)

19. Bernard, Jessie S. The Female World (New York: Collier-Macmillan, 1981)

20. Bernard, Jessie. Women and the Public Interest: An Essay on Policy and Protest (Chicago: Aldine-Atherton, 1971)

21. Bernard, Jessie S. and Calfred B. Broderick. The Individual, Sex, and Society (Baltimore, MD: Johns Hopkins University Press, 1969)

22. "The Black Women's Issue," Conditions, Vol. 5 (1979)

23. "Blacks and the Sexual Revolution [Symposium]," Black Scholar, Vol. 9 (April 1978), pp. 2-56

24. Boals, Kay. "The Politics of Cultural Liberation," Women in Politics, Jaquette, Jane S., ed. (New York: Wiley, 1974), pp. 322-342

25. Boles, Janet K. The Policies of the Equal Rights Amendment: Conflict and the Decision Process (New York: Longman, 1979)

26. Bond, J. C. and C. E. Gregory. "Two Views of Black Macho and the Myth of the Superwoman (Review Article)," Freedomways, Vol. 19, No. 1 (1979), pp. 13-26

27. Boulding, E. "Women and Social Violence," International Social Science Journal, Vol. 30, No. 4 (1978), pp. 801-815

28. Brown, Barbara A; Ann E. Freedman; Harriet N. Katz; and Alice M. Price. Women's Rights and the Law: The Impact of the ERA on State Laws (New York: Praeger Publishers, 1977)

29. Brown, D. R. and W. F. Anderson. "Survey of the Black Woman and the Persuasion Process: The Study of Strategies of Identification and Resistance,"

Journal of Black Studies, Vol. 9 (December 1978),
pp. 233-248

30. Cade, Toni, ed. The Black Woman (New York:
Bobbs-Merrill, 1970)

31. Cagan, E. "Selling of the Women's Movement,"
Social Policy, Vol. 9 (May 1978), pp. 4-12

32. Cancian, F. M. and B. L. Ross. "Mass Media and
the Women's Movement: 1900-1977," Journal of
Applied Behavioural Science, Vol. 17, No. 1
(1981), pp. 9-26

33. Cantor, Milton and Bruce Laurie. Class, Sex, and
the Woman Worker, Introduction by Caroline I. Ware
(Westport, CT: Greenwood Press, 1977)

34. Carden, Maren Lockwood. The New Feminist Movement
(New York: Russell Sage, 1974)

35. Carroll, Bernice A. "Political Science, Part II:
International Politics, Comparative Politics, and
Feminist Radicals," Signs, Vol. 5 (Spring 1980),
pp. 449-458

36. Cassell, Joan. A Group Called Women: Symbolism
in the Feminist Movement (New York: David McKay
Company, Inc., 1977)

37. Chafe, William H. Women and Equality: Changing
Patterns in American Culture (Oxford: Oxford
University Press, 1977)

38. "Chicanas in the National Landscape," Frontiers,
Vol. 5 (Summer 1980), Special Issue

39. Chisholm, Shirley. "Racism and Anti-Feminism,"
Black Scholar, Vol. 1 (Jan.-Feb. 1970), pp. 40-45

40. Cohen, S. M. "American Jewish Feminism: A Study
in Conflicts and Compromises," American Behavioral
Science, Vol. 23 (March 1980), pp. 519-558

41. Colon, Clara. Enter Fighting: Today's Woman: A Marxist-Leninist View (New York: New Outlook Publishers, 1970)

42. "Controversy Over the 'Equal Rights for Women' Amendment [U.S.]: Pro & Con," Congressional Digest, Vol. 50 (January 1971), pp. 1-32

43. Cook, Blanche. "Female Support Networks and Political Activism," Chrysalis, No. 3 (1977), pp. 43-61

44. Costain, A. N. "Representing Women: The Transition from Social Movement to Interest Group," Western Political Quarterly, Vol. 34 (March 1981), pp. 100-112

45. Costain, A. N. "Struggle for a National Women's Lobby: Organizing a Diffuse Interest," Western Political Quarterly, Vol. 33 (December 1980), pp. 476-491

46. Curtis, Russell L. and Louis A. Zurcher. "Social Movements: An Analytical Exploration of Organizational Forms," Social Problems, Vol. 21 (April 1973), pp. 356-370

47. Daniels, Gabrielle. "First Black Lesbian Conference," Off Our Backs, Vol. 10 (December 1980), pp. 4-5

48. Davis, Angela Y. Women, Race and Class (New York: Random House, 1982)

49. Davis, J. C. "On the Measurement of Discrimination Against Women," American Journal of Economics and Sociology, Vol. 38 (July 1979), pp. 287-292

50. Davis, M. "Modern Feminism and Women's Organization," World Marxist Review, Vol. 24 (July 1981), pp. 73-76

51. Deckard, Barbara Sinclair. The Women's Movement:
    Political, Socioeconomic, and Psychological Issues
    (New York: Harper & Row, Publishers, 1979)

52. Dill, Bonnie Thorton. "The Dialectics of Black
    Womanhood," Signs, Vol. 4 (Spring 1979), pp.
    543-555

53. DuBois, Ellen, ed. Elizabeth Cady Stanton/Susan
    B. Anthony: Correspondence, Writings, Speeches
    (New York: Schocken Books, 1981)

54. Dworkin, Andrea. Right-wing Women (New York:
    Perigee Books, 1983)

55. Dworkin, Andrea. "Safety, Shelter, Rules, Form,
    Love: The Promise of the Ultra-Right," Ms., Vol.
    7 (June 1979), pp. 62-64

56. Editorial Research Reports on the Women's Movement
    (Washington, DC: Congressional Quarterly, 1973)

57. Editorial Research Reports on the Women's
    Movement: Achievements and Effects (Washington,
    DC: Congressional Quarterly, 1977)

58. Editorial Research Reports on the Women's
    Movement: Agenda for the '80s. (Washington, DC:
    Congressional Quarterly, 1981)

59. Elsasser, Nan; Kyle MacKenzie; and Yvonne Tixier y
    Vigil. Las Mujeres: Conversations from a
    Hispanic Community (Old Westbury, NY: Feminist
    Press, 1980)

60. Enloe, Cynthia. "Women--The Reserve Army of Army
    Labor (Ideological Processes That Shape Three
    Spheres of Women's Military Use: As Soldiers, As
    Defense Industry Laborers, As Mothers of Future
    Soldiers)," Review of Radical Political Economy,
    Vol. 12 (Summer 1980), pp. 43-52

61. Enriquez, Evangelina. La Chicana: The Mexican-
    American Woman (Chicago: University of Chicago
    Press, 1979) (see also Mirande, Alfredo, entry
    137)

62. Epstein, Cynthia Fuchs. Woman's Place (Berkeley,
    CA: University of California Press, 1971)

63. Evans, Judith. "Women and Politics: A
    Re-appraisal," Political Studies, Vol. 28 (June
    1980), pp. 210-221

64. Evans, Sara. Personal Politics: The Roots of the
    Feminist Movement in the Civil Rights Movement and
    New Left (New York: Random House, 1979)

65. "Feminism: The Road Ahead," Atlas, Vol. 25 (April
    1978), pp. 31-37

66. Ferree, Myra. "Working Class Feminism: A
    Consideration of the Consequences of Employment,"
    Sociological Quarterly, Vol. 21 (Spring 1980), pp.
    173-184

67. Firestone, Shulamith. The Dialectic of Sex (New
    York.: William Morrow, 1970)

68. Fisher, B. "Models Among Us: Social Authority
    and Political Activism," Feminist Studies, Vol. 7
    (Spring 1981), pp. 100-112

69. Fishman, Walda Katz. The New Right: Unravelling
    the Opposition to Women's Equality (New York:
    Praeger, 1982)

70. Forisha, Barbara L. and Barbara H. Goldman.
    Outsiders on the Inside: Women and Organizations
    (New York: Prentice-Hall, 1981)

71. Fowler, Marguerite Gilbert. "Feminism and
    Political Radicalism," Journal of Psychology, Vol.
    83 (1973), pp. 237-242

72. Fox, Bonnie, ed. Hidden in the Household:
    Women's Domestic Labour Under Capitalism (Toronto:
    Women's Educational Press, 1980)

73. Freeman, Jo. The Politics of Women's Liberation:
    A Case Study of an Emerging Social Movement and
    its Relation to the Public Policy Process (New
    York: Longman, 1975)

74. Freeman, Jo. "Crises and Conflicts In Social
    Movement Organizations," Chrysalis, Vol. 5 (1978),
    pp. 45-51

75. Freeman, Jo. "The Building of the Gilded Cage,"
    Radical Feminism, Koedt, Anne; Ellen Levine; and
    Anita Rapone, eds. (New York: Quadrangle, 1973),
    pp. 127-150

76. Friedan, Betty. It Changed My Life: Writings on
    the Women's Movement (New York: Random House,
    1976)

77. Friedan, Betty. The Feminine Mystique (New York:
    Norton, 1963; 2nd ed. 1974)

78. Friedan, Betty. The Second Stage (New York:
    Summit Books, 1981)

79. Fritz, Leah. Dreamers and Dealers: An Intimate
    Appraisal of the Women's Movement (Boston: Beacon
    Press, 1979)

80. Fulenwider, Claire Knoche. Feminism in American
    Politics: A Study of Ideological Influence (New
    York: Praeger, 1980)

81. Garrison, Dee. "From Private Vice to Public
    Virtue: The Birth Control Movement and American
    Society," Journal of Social History, Vol. 12
    (Summer 1979), pp. 651-653

82. Gelb, Joyce and Marian Lief Palley. "Women and
    Interest Group Politics: A Case Study of the

Equal Credit Opportunity Act," American Politics Quarterly, Vol. 5 (July 1977), pp. 331-352

83. Gelb, Joyce and Marian Lief Palley. Women and Public Policies (Princeton, NJ: Princeton University Press, 1982)

84. Giele, Janet Zollinger. "Revolution in Sex Roles," "Sex Roles, Politics, and Liberation," in her Women and the Future: Changing Sex Roles in Modern America (New York: The Free Press, 1978), pp. 1-86

85. Gilder, George F. "Sex and the Social Order: Politics Hidden Dimension (Dissection of Current Feminist Ideas)," New Leader, Vol. 56 (September 3, 1973), pp. 5-10

86. Goldstein, Leslie Friedman. The Constitutional Rights of Women: Cases in Law and Social Change (New York: Longman, 1979)

87. Gonzales, Sylvia. "La Chicana: Guadalupe or Malinche," Comparative Perspectives of Third World Women: The Impact of Sex, Race and Class, Lindsay, Beverly, ed. (New York: Praeger, 1980), pp. 229-250)

88. Gonzales, Sylvia. "The White Feminist Movement: The Chicana Perspective," Social Science Journal, Vol. 14 (April 1977), pp. 67-76

89. Goodes, W. J. "Why Men Resist," Dissent, Vol. 27 (Spring 1980), pp. 181-193

90. Gordon, Linda. Women's Body, Woman's Right: A Social History of Birth Control in America (New York: Viking, 1976)

91. Gornick, Vivian and Barbara K. Moran. eds. Women in Sexist Society: Studies in Power and Powerlessness (New York: Basic Books, 1971)

92. Green, P. "Feminist Consciousness," Sociological Quarterly, Vol. 20 (Summer 1979), pp. 359-374

93. Gruenebaum, Jane. "Women in Politics (Movements by American Women to Attain Equal Rights, Suffrage and Full Equality, 1940 to the Present)," Academy of Political Science, Proceedings, Vol. 34, No. 2 (1981), pp. 104-120

94. Gurko, Miriam. The Ladies of Seneca Falls: The Birth of the Woman's Rights Movement (New York: Schocken Books, 1976)

95. Hall, Gus. Working-Class Approach to Women's Liberation (New York: New Outlook Publishers, 1970)

96. Handler, Joel. Social Movements and the Legal System: A Theory of Law Reform and Social Change (New York: Academic Press, 1978)

97. Hartsock, Nancy. "Political Change: Two Perspectives on Power," Quest: A Feminist Quarterly, Vol. 1 (Summer 1974), pp. 10-25

98. Heer, D. M. and A. Grossbard-Shechtman. "Impact of the Female Marriage Squeeze and the Contraceptive Revolution on Sex Roles and the Women's Liberation Movement in the United States, 1960 to 1975," Journal of Marriage and the Family, Vol. 43 (February 1981), pp. 49-65

99. Heiskanen, Veronica Stolte. "Sex Roles, Social Class and Political Consciousness," Acta Sociologica, Vol. 14, Nos. 1-2 (1971), pp. 83-95

100. Hole, Judith and Ellen Levine. Rebirth of Feminism (New York: Quandrangle Books, 1971)

101. Holter, Harriet. "Sex Roles and Social Change," Acta Sociologica, Vol. 14, Nos. 1-2 (1971), pp. 2-12

102. Hooks, Bell. Ain't I a Woman: Black Women and
     Feminism (Boston: South End Press, 1981)

103. Huck, S. L. M. "Five Million Dollar
     Misunderstanding [National Women's Convention,
     Houston, November 18-21, 1977]," American
     Opinion, Vol. 21 (January 1978), pp. 1-4

104. Iglitzin, Lynne B. "Political Education and
     Sexual Liberation," Politics and Society, Vol. 2
     (Winter 1972), pp. 241-254

105. Janeway, Elizabeth. Powers of the Weak (New
     York: Knopf Publishers, 1980)

106. Janeway, Elizabeth. "The Weak are the Second
     Sex," Atlantic Monthly, Vol. 232 (December 1973),
     pp. 91-104

107. Jaquette, Jane S., ed. Women in Politics (New
     York: John Wiley and Sons, 1975)

108. Jarrard, Mary W. "Emerging ERA (Equal Rights
     Amendment) Patterns in Editorial in Southern
     Daily Newspapers: Conservative Rhetoric Evident
     in Editorials in Newspapers from 1970 to 1977,"
     Journalism Quarterly, Vol 57 (Winter 1980), pp.
     606-611.

109. Johnston, Jill. Lesbian Nation: The Feminist
     Solution (New York: Simon and Schuster, 1973)

110. Joseph, Gloria I. and Jill Lewis. Common
     Differences: Conflicts in Black and White
     Feminist Perspectives (New York: Anchor Press,
     1981)

111. Joyce, Rosemary O. A Woman's Place: The Life
     History of a Rural Ohio Grandmother (Columbus,
     OH: Ohio State University Press, 1982)

112. Justice, Betty and Renate Pore, eds. Toward the
     Second Decade: The Impact of the Women's

Movement on American Institutions (Westport, CT: Greenwood Press, 1981)

113. Kikumura, Akemi. Through Harsh Winters: The Life of a Japanese Immigrant Woman (Novato, CA: Chandler and Sharp, 1981)

114. Kimball, Gayle, ed. Women's Culture: The Women's Renaissance of the Seventies (Metuchen, NJ: Scarecrow Press, 1981)

115. Kirschten, Dick. "Reagan's Approach to Women's Issues—Let Them Simmer on the Back Burner: The President Has Appointed Few Women to Top Posts in His Administration, and He Has Been Slow to Support Legislative Proposals to Eliminate Sex Discrimination," National Journal, Vol. 13 (May 23, 1981), pp. 926-927

116. Koedt, Anne; Ellen Levine; and Anita Rapone, eds. Radical Feminism (New York: Quadrangle Books, 1973)

117. Kolodney, N. "Semantics of the Women's Liberation Movement," ETC, Vol. 35 (September 1978), pp. 298-301

118. Koltun, Elizabeth, ed. The Jewish Woman: New Perspectives (New York: Schocken Books, 1976)

119. Krichmar, Albert. The Women's Movement in the 1970s: An International English Language Bibliography (Metuchen, NJ: Scarecrow Press, 1977)

120. Lavine, T. Z. "Ideas of Revolution in the Women's Movement," American Behavioral Scientist, Vol. 20 (March 1977), pp. 535-566

121. Lavrin, Asuncion, ed. Latin American Women: Historical Perspectives (Westport, CT: Greenwood Press, 1978)

122. Lewis, Sasha Gregory. Sunday's Women (Boston: Beacon Press, 1979)

123. Lindsay, Beverly, ed. Comparative Perspectives of Third World Women: The Impact of Race, Sex, and Class (New York: Praeger Publishers, 1980) (Includes Research on Native American, Chicana, Black and Vietnamese Women)

124. Lindsay, Beverly. "Minority Women in America," The Study of Women: Enlarging Perspectives of Social Reality, Snyder, Eloise C., ed. (New York: Harper & Row, 1979), pp. 318-363

125. Lines, Amelia Akehurst. To Raise Myself a Little: The Diaries and Letters of Jennie, a Georgia Teacher, 1851-1886, Dyer, Thomas, ed. (Athens, GA: University of Georgia Press, 1981, c. 1947)

126. Lipman-Blumen, Jean. "How Ideology Shapes Women's Lives," Scientific American, Vol. 226. (January 1972), pp. 34-42

127. Lipman-Blumen, Jean. "Role De-Differentiation as a System Response to Crisis: Occupational and Political Roles of Women," Sociological Inquiry, Vol. 43, No. 2 (1973), pp. 105-129

128. McCarthy, John D. and Mayer N. Zald. "Resource Mobilization and Social Movements: A Partial Theory" American Journal of Sociology, Vol. 82 (May 1977), pp. 1212-1241

129. McClain, E. "Feminists and Non-feminists: Contrasting Profiles in Independence and Affiliation," Psychological Report, Vol. 43 (October 1978), pp. 435-441

130. McWilliams, Nancy. "Contemporary Feminism, Consciousness-Raising and Changing Views of the Political," Women in Politics, Jaquette, Jane S., ed. (New York: Wiley, 1974), pp. 157-170

131. Mandle, Joan D. Women and Social Change in
     America (Princeton, NJ: Princeton Book Company,
     1979)

132. Mandle, Joan D. "Women's Liberation: Humanizing
     Rather than Polarizing," Annals of the American
     Academy of Political and Social Science, Vol. 397
     (September 1971), pp. 118-128

133. Masi, Dale A. Organizing for Women: Issues,
     Strategies, and Services (Lexington, MA: D. C.
     Heath and Company, 1981)

134. Mauss, Armand L. and Julie Camille Wolfe, eds.
     This Land of Promises: the Rise and Fall of
     Social Problems (New York: J. B. Lippincott Co.,
     1977)

135. Messner, E. "Unconscious Source of Opposition to
     the Liberation of Women," American Journal of
     Orthopsychiatry, Vol. 49 (January 1979), pp.
     161-163

136. Miner, Valerie. "Indian Women and the Indian
     Act: When Women's Rights and the Indian Rights
     Collide, Who Wins? The Answer Isn't Easy,"
     (Canada) Saturday Night, Vol. 89 (April 1974),
     pp. 28-31

137. Mirande, Alfredo and Evangelina Enriquez. La
     Chicana: The Mexican-American Woman (Chicago:
     University of Chicago Press, 1980)

138. Mitchell, Juliet. Women's Estate (New York:
     Pantheon Books, 1972)

139. Moreno, Dorinda. "Chicana Activist Speaks,"
     UNION W.A.G.E., Vol. 59 (May-June 1980), p. 7

140. Morgan, Robin. Going Too Far: The Personal
     Chronicle of a Feminist (New York: A Vintage
     Book, 1982)

141. Morgan, Robin, ed. Sisterhood Is Powerful: An
     Anthology of Writings from the Women's Liberation
     Movement (New York: Vintage, 1970)

142. Morris, Monica. "The Public Definition of Social
     Movements: Women's Liberation,"
     Sociology and Social Research, Vol. 51 (July
     1973), pp. 526-543

143. Newland, Kathleen. The Sisterhood of Man (New
     York: W.W. Norton and Co., 1979)

144. Nicholson, Linda J. "Personal is Political: An
     Analysis in Retrospect," Social Theory and
     Practice, Vol. 7 (May 18, 1982), pp. 85-98

145. Oakley, Ann. Subject Women (New York: Pantheon,
     1981)

146. O'Connor, Karen. Women's Organizations' Use of
     the Courts (Lexington, MA: Lexington Books,
     1980)

147. Off Our Backs: Special Issue on Racism and
     Sexism, Vol. 10. (November 1979)

148. O'Neill, William L. Everyone Was Brave: A
     History of Feminism in America (Chicago:
     Quadrangle Books, 1969)

149. Papachristou, Judith. Women Together: A History
     in Documents of the Women's Movement in the
     United States (New York: Knopf Books, 1976)

150. Petchesky, Rosalind. "Antiabortion, Antifeminism
     and the Rise of the New Right," Feminist Studies,
     Vol. 7 (Summer 1981), pp. 206-246

151. Piven, Frances Fox and Richard A. Cloward. Poor
     People's Movements: Why They Succeed, How They
     Fail (New York: Random House, 1979)

152. The Political Economy of Women, Review of Radical
     Political Economy, Vol. 12 (Summer 1980), pp.
     1-94, fourth special issue

153. Ponse, Barbara. Identities in the Lesbian World
     (Westport, CT: Greenwood Press, 1978)

154. Puryear, Gwendolyn Randall. "The Black Woman:
     Liberated or Oppressed?," Comparative
     Perspectives of Third World Women: The Impact of
     Sex, Race and Class, Lindsay, Beverly, ed. (New
     York: Praeger Publishers, 1980), pp. 251-275

155. Reed, Evelyn. Problems of Women's Liberation: A
     Marxist Approach (New York: Merit Publishers,
     1972, c. 1970)

156. Reid, Inez Smith. "Together" Black Women,
     prepared for the Black Women's Community
     Development Foundation (New York: Third Press,
     1975)

157. Rendel, Margherita, ed. Women, Power and
     Political Systems (New York: St. Martin's Press,
     1981)

158. Rich, Adrienne. "Compulsory Heterosexuality and
     Lesbian Experience," Signs, Vol. 5 (Summer 1980),
     pp. 631-660

159. Robey, J. S. et al. "America's State Policies
     and the Women's Movement," State Government, Vol.
     54, No. 2 (1981), pp. 58-64

160. Rogers, S. C. "Woman's Place: A Critical Review
     of Anthropological Theory," Comparative Study of
     Society and History, Vol. 20 (January 1978), pp.
     123-162

161. Romer, Karen T. and Cynthia Secor. "The Time is
     Here for Women's Liberation," Annals of the
     American Academy of Political and Social Science,
     Vol. 397 (September 1971), pp. 129-139

162. Ross, Loretta J. "Black Women Ponder: Why
     Feminism?," New Directions for Women, Vol. 10
     (July-August 1981), pp. 5ff.

163. Ross, Pearl. "Feminism as Balance: A Committed
     Humanist Has Gained New Insight Into Helping
     Males Understand the Women's Movement," Humanist,
     Vol. 40 (March-April 1980), pp. 31-33

164. Rowbotham, Sheila. Women, Resistance and
     Revolution: A History of Women and Revolution in
     the Modern Age (New York: Vintage Books, 1974)

165. Rowbotham, Sheila; Lynn Segal; and Hilary
     Wainwright. Beyond the Fragments: Feminism and
     the Making of Socialism (London: Islington
     Community Press, 1979)

166. Sandoval, Che. "Hispanic Feminist Conference
     Meets," La Razon Mestiza/UNION W.A.G.E., Vol. 60
     (June 1980), pp. 4-5

167. Sapiro, Virginia. "News From the Front:
     Intersex and Intergenerational Conflict Over the
     Status of Women," Western Political Quarterly,
     Vol. 33 (June 1980), pp. 260-270

168. Scharf, Lois. To Work and to Wed: Female
     Employment, Feminism, and the Great Depression
     (Westport, CT: Greenwood Press, 1980)

169. Sedwick, Catherine and R. Williams. "Black Women
     and the Equal Rights Amendment," Black Scholar,
     Vol. 7 (July-August 1976), pp. 24-29

170. Seifer, Nancy. Absent From the Majority:
     Working Class Women in America (New York:
     American Jewish Committee, Institute on Human
     Relations, 1973)

171. Shear, Marie. "Stoolies, Ciphers, and Alibis:
     Women in the White House Transcripts," ETC., Vol.
     33 (March 1976), pp. 88-92

172. Sigel, R. S. and J. V. Reynolds. "Generational
     Differences and the Women's Movement," Political
     Science Quarterly, Vol. 94 (Winter 1979-1980),
     pp. 635-648

173. Simpson, Ruth. From the Closets to the Courts
     (New York: Penguin Books, 1976)

174. Skrabanek, Robert L. "The Growing Power of Women
     (Numerical, Economic, Political)," American
     Demographics, Vol. 2 (September 1980), pp. 22-25

175. Snyder, Eloise C. "The Anatomy of the Women's
     Social Movement," in her The Study of Women:
     Enlarging Perspectives of Social Reality (New
     York: Harper & Row, 1979), pp. 13-39

176. Solomon, Martha. "The Rhetoric of STOP ERA:
     Fatalistic Reaffirmation," Southern Speech
     Communication Journal, Vol. 44 (Fall 1978), pp.
     42-59

177. Spector, Malcolm and John I. Kitsuse. "Social
     Problems: A Re-Formulation," Social Problems,
     Vol. 21 (Fall 1973), pp. 145-159

178. Stacey, Margaret and Marion Price. Women, Power,
     and Politics (London: Tavistock Publications,
     1981)

179. Stember, Charles Herbert. Sexual Racism: The
     Emotional Barrier to an Integrated Society (New
     York: Greenwood Press, 1976)

180. Stewart, Debra W. The Women's Movement in
     Community Politics in the U.S.: The Role of
     Local Commissions on the Status of Women (New
     York: Pergamon Press, 1980)

181. Stimpson, Catherine. R. "Neither Dominant Nor
     Subordinate: The Women's Movement and
     Contemporary American Culture," Dissent, Vol. 27
     (Summer 1980), pp. 299-307

182. Strauss, Sylvia. "Traitors to the Masculine
     Cause:" The Men's Campaigns for Women's Rights
     (Westport, CT: Greenwood Press, 1982)

183. Tax, Meredith. "Woman and Her Mind: The Story
     of Everyday Life," Radical Feminism, Koedt, Anne;
     Ellen Levine; and Anita Rapone, eds. (New York:
     Quadrangle, 1973), pp. 23-35

184. Thomas, L. "Sexism and Racism: Some Conceptual
     Differences," Ethics, Vol. 90 (January 1980), pp.
     239-256

185. Tilly, Louise. A. "Social Sciences and the Study
     of Women," Comparative Study of Society and
     History, Vol. 20 (January 1978), pp. 163-173

186. Tripp, Maggie, ed. Women in the Year 2000 (New
     York: Arbor House, 1974)

187. United States Congress, House of Representatives,
     Committee on Education and Labor, Subcommittee on
     Employment Opportunities. Civil Rights
     Amendments Act of 1979: Hearing on H.R. 2074 to
     Prohibit Discrimination on the Basis of
     Affectional or Sexual Orientation, and for Other
     Purposes, 96th Congress, 2nd Session, October 10,
     1980 (Washington, DC: U.S. Government Printing
     Office, 1980)

188. United States Congress, House of Representatives,
     Committee on the Judiciary, Subcommittee No. 4
     Equal Rights for Men and Women 1971: Hearings on
     H. J. res. 35 [and] 208 and related bills and H.
     R. 916 and related bills. 92nd Congress, 1st
     Session, March 24-April 5, 1971 (Washington, DC:
     U.S. Government Printing Office, 1971)

189. United States Congress, Senate, Committee on the
     Judiciary. Equal Rights 1970: Hearings on S. J.
     res. 61 and S. J. res. 231, 91st Congress, 2nd

Session, September 9-15, 1970 (Washington, DC:
U.S. Government Printing Office, 1970)

190. United States Congress, Senate, Committee on the
Judiciary, Subcommittee on Constitutional
Amendments. The "Equal Rights" Amendment:
Hearings on S. J. res 61, 91st Congress, 2nd
Session, May 5-7, 1970 (Washington, DC: U.S.
Government Printing Office, 1970)

191. United States National Committee on the
Observance of International Women's Year. The
Spirit of Houston: The First National Women's
Conference: An Official Report to the President,
the Congress and the People of the United States
(Washington, DC: U.S. Government Printing
Office, March 1978)

192. United States Presidential Advisory Committee for
Women. Voices for Women: 1980 Report
(Washington, DC: U.S. Government Printing
Office, 1980)

193. Vida, Ginny, ed. Our Right to Love: A Lesbian
Resource Book (New York: Prentice-Hall
Publishers, 1978)

194. Wallace, Michele. Black Macho and the Myth of
the Superwoman (New York: Dial Press, 1979)

195. Warenski, Marilyn. Patriarchs and Politics: The
Plight of the Mormon Women (New York:
McGraw-Hill Book Co., 1978)

196. Watkins, Mel. To Be A Black Woman (New York:
William Morrow, 1970)

197. Weber, Shirley N. "Black Power in the 1960s: A
Study of its Impact on Women's Liberation,"
Journal of Black Studies, Vol. 11 (June 1981),
pp. 483-498

Social Movements   21

198. West, Guida. The National Welfare Rights
     Movement: The Social Protest of Poor Women (New
     York: Praeger Publishers, 1981)

199. Witt, S. H. "Brave-hearted Women: The Struggle
     at Wounded Knee," Civil Rights Digest, Vol. 8
     (Summer 1976), pp. 38-45

200. Wittstock, Laura Waterman. "Native American
     Women: Twilight of a Long Maidenhood,"
     Comparative Perspectives of Third World Women:
     The Impact of Sex, Race and Class, Lindsay,
     Beverly, ed. (New York: Praeger Publishers,
     1980), pp. 207-228

201. Wolf, Deborah Goleman. The Lesbian Community
     (Berkeley, CA: University of California Press,
     1979)

202. "Women and the Church," Dialogue, Vol. 10 (Spring
     1971), Special Issue

203. "Women, Class and the Family: Third Special
     Issue on the Political Economy of Women," Review
     of Radical Political Economy, Vol. 9 (Fall 1977),
     pp. 1-78

II. POLITICAL AND SOCIAL HISTORY OF FEMINISM AND
WOMEN'S RIGHTS IN THE U.S.

204. Anderson, Karen. Wartime Women: Sex Roles,
Family Relations, and the Status of Women During
World War II (Westport, CT: Greenwood Press,
1981)

205. Anthony, Susan B. and Ida Husted Harper, eds.,
History of Women Suffrage, Vol. 4 (Indianapolis,
IN: Hollenbeck Press, 1902)

206. Aptheker, Bettina. Woman's Legacy: Essays on
Race, Sex, and Class in American History
(Amherst, MA: University of Massachusetts Press,
1982)

207. Armitage, Susan. "Western Women's History: A
Review Essay," Frontiers, Vol. 5 (Fall 1980), pp.
71-73

208. Baer, Judith A. The Chains of Protection: The
Judicial Response to Women's Labor Legislation
(Westport, CT: Greenwood Press, 1978)

209. Barker-Benfield, Graham John. Horrors of the
Half-Known Life: Male Attitudes Toward Women and
Sexuality in Nineteenth Century America, (New
York: Harper & Row, 1976)

210. Basch, Norma. In the Eyes of the Law: Women,
Marriage and Property in Nineteenth Century New
York (Ithaca, NY: Cornell University Press,
1982)

211. Baxandall, Rosalyn; Linda Gordon; and Susan
     Reverby, eds. America's Working Women: A
     Documentary History--1600 to the Present (New
     York: Vintage, 1976)

212. Beard, Mary Ritter. Woman as a Force in History
     (New York: Collier Books, 1972), reprint of 1946
     edition

213. Beard, Mary Ritter, ed. America Through Women's
     Eyes (New York: Macmillan, 1933)

214. Becker, Susan D. The Origins of the Equal Rights
     Amendment: American Feminism Between the Wars
     (Westport, CT: Greenwood Press, 1981)

215. Benson, Ronald M. "Searching for the Antecedents
     of Affirmative Action: The National War Labor
     Board and the Cleveland Women Conductors in World
     War I," Women's Rights Law Reporter, Vol. 5
     (Summer 1979), pp. 271-282

216. Berg, Barbara. The Remembered Gate: Origins of
     American Feminism (Oxford: Oxford University
     Press, 1978)

217. Bernikow, Louise. Among Women (New York:
     Harmony Books, 1980)

218. Breen, W. J. "Black Women and the Great War:
     Mobilization and Reform in the South," Journal of
     Southern History, Vol. 44 (August 1978), pp.
     421-440

219. Campbell, Helen Stuart. Prisoners of Poverty:
     Women Wage-Workers, Their Trades and Their Lives
     (Boston: Greenwood Press, 1972) reprint of 1887
     edition

220. Carden, Maren Lockwood. The New Feminist
     Movement (New York: Russell Sage Foundation,
     1974)

221. Cassell, Joan. A Group Called Women: Sisterhood and Symbolism in the Feminist Movement (New York: David McKay Company, Inc., 1977)

222. Chafe, William H. The American Woman: Her Changing Social, Economic, and Political Roles, 1920-1970 (New York: Oxford University Press, 1972)

223. Chafe, William H. "An Historical Overview," in his Women and Equality: Changing Patterns in American Culture (New York: Oxford University Press, 1977), pp. 13-42

224. Cott, Nancy F. "Liberation Politics in Two Eras: Review Essay," American Quarterly, Vol. 32 (Spring 1980), pp. 96-105

225. Cott, Nancy F. and Elizabeth Pleck, eds. A Heritage of Her Own: Toward a New Social History of American Women (New York: Simon and Schuster, 1979)

226. Cott, Nancy F., ed. The Root of Bitterness: Documents of the Social History of American Women (New York: Dutton, 1972)

227. Cumbler, J. T. "Politics of Charity: Gender and Class in the Late 19th Century Charity Policy," Journal of Social History, Vol. 14 (Fall 1980), pp. 99-111

228. Dawson, Deborah A. "Fertility Control in the United States Before the Contraceptive Revolution," Family Planning Perspectives, Vol. 12 (March-April 1980), pp. 76-78f

229. Deckard, Barbara. "A Century of Struggle: American Women 1820-1920," "Forty Years in the Desert: American Women, 1920-1960," "The New Struggle for Liberation: American Women, 1960 to the Present," "Current Issues of the Women's

Movement," in her The Women's Movement (New York: Harper & Row, 1979)

230. Deutrich, Mabel E. and Virginia C. Purdy, eds. Clio Was a Woman: Studies in the History of American Women (Washington, DC: Howard University Press 1980)

231. Douglas, Ann. The Feminization of American Culture (New York: Avon, 1977)

232. Douglass, Frederick. Frederick Douglass on Women's Rights, Foner, Philip S., ed. (Westport, CT: Greenwood Press, 1976)

233. DuBois, Ellen. Feminism and Suffrage: The Emergence of an Independent Women's Movement in America, 1848-1869 (Ithaca, NY: Cornell University Press, 1978)

234. DuBois, Ellen. "The Nineteenth-Century Woman Suffrage Movement and the Analysis of Women's Oppression," Capitalist Patriarchy and the Case for Socialist Feminism, Eisenstein, Zillah (New York: Monthly Review, 1979), pp. 137-150

235. Ellsworth, Edward W. Liberators of the Female Mind: The Shirreff Sisters, Educational Reform, and the Women's Movement (Westport, CT: Greenwood Press, 1979)

236. Evans, Sara. Personal Politics: The Roots of Women's Liberation in the Civil Rights Movement and the New Left (New York: Random House, 1979)

237. Ferree, Myra. "Working Class Feminisim: A Consideration of the Consequences of Employment," Sociological Quarterly, Vol. 21 (Spring 1980), pp. 173-184

238. Flexner, Eleanor. Century of Struggle (New York: Antheneum, 1974)

239. Freedman, Estelle B. "The New Woman: Changing
     Views of Women in the 1920s," Journal of American
     History, Vol. 61 (October 1974), pp. 372-393

240. Freeman, Jo. The Politics of Women's Liberation:
     A Case Study of an Emerging Social Movement and
     its Relation to the Public Policy Process (New
     York: David McKay Co., 1975)

241. Freeman, Jo. "The Women's Liberation Movement:
     Its Origins, Structures, Impact, and Ideas,"
     Women: A Feminist Perspective, Freeman, Jo ed.
     (Palo Alto, CA: Mayfield, 1975), pp. 448-460

242. Freeman, Jo. "Origins of the Women's Liberation
     Movement," American Journal of Sociology, Vol. 78
     (January 1973), pp. 792-811

243. Friedman, Jean E. and William G. Shade, eds. Our
     American Sisters: Women in American Life and
     Thought (Lexington, MA: D.C. Heath and Company,
     1982, Third Edition)

244. Gabin, N. "Women Workers and the UAW in the
     Post-World War II Period: 1945-1954," Labor
     History, Vol. 21 (Winter 1979-80), pp. 5-30

245. Garcia, M. T. "Chicana in American History: The
     Mexican Women of El Paso, 1880-1920--A Case
     Study," Pacific Historical Review, Vol. 49 (May
     1980), pp. 315-337

246. Garrison, Dee. "From Private Vice to Public
     Virtue: The Birth Control Movement and American
     Society," Journal of Social History, Vol. 12
     (Summer 1979), pp. 651-653

247. Geidel, P. "National Women's Party and the
     Origins of the Equal Rights Amendment,
     1920-1923," Historian, Vol. 42 (August 1980), pp.
     557-582

248. Gordon, A.; M. J. Buhle; and N. Schram. "Women in American Society: A Historical Contribution," Radical America, Vol. 5 (July-Aug. 1971), pp. 3-66

249. Gordon, Linda. Woman's Body, Woman's Right: A Social History Of Birth Control in America (New York: Viking, 1976)

250. Graebner, W. "Uncle Sam Just Loves the Ladies: Sex Discrimination in the Federal Government, 1917," Labor History, Vol. 21 (Winter 1979-1980), pp. 75-85

251. Greenwald, Maurine Weiner. Women, War, and Work: The Impact of World War I on Women Workers in the United States (Westport, CT: Greenwood Press, 1980)

252. Gurko, Miriam. The Ladies of Seneca Falls: The Birth of the Woman's Rights Movement (New York: Schocken Books, 1976)

253. Guzda, Henry P. "Francis Perkin's Interest in a New Deal for Blacks: The Black Oriented Programs of the Nation's First Female Cabinet Member May Seem Modest by Today's Standards; However, in Her Time She Was a Pioneer, Who Made the Welfare of Blacks A Priority of the Department of Labor," Monthly Labor Review, Vol. 103 (April 1980), pp. 31-35

254. Hales, J. G. "Co-laborers in the Cause: Women in the Antebellum Nativist Movement," Civil War History, Vol. 25 (June 1979), pp. 119-138

255. Harris, Barbara J. Beyond Her Sphere: Women and the Professions in American History (Westport, CT: Greenwood Press, 1978)

256. Hartman, Mary S. and Lois W. Banner, eds. Clio's Consciousness Raised: New Perspectives on the History of Women (New York: Octagon Books, 1976)

257. Hayden, Dolores. The Grand Domestic Revolution:
     A History of Feminist Designs for American Homes,
     Neighbourhoods, and Cities (Cambridge, MA: The
     MIT Press, 1981)

258. Hill, Joseph Adna. Women in Gainful Occupations,
     1870 to 1920 (New York: Johnson Reprint
     Corporation, 1972) reprinted from U.S. Government
     Printing Office, 1907

259. Hole, Judith and Ellen Levine. "The First
     Feminists," Radical Feminism, Koedt, Anne; Ellen
     Levine; and Anita Rapone, eds. (New York:
     Quadrangle, 1973), pp. 3-16

260. Hole, Judith and Ellen Levine. Rebirth of
     Feminism (New York: Quadrangle, 1971)

261. Hollis, Patricia. "Working Women," History, Vol.
     62 (October 1977), pp. 439-445

262. Ichioka, Yuji. "Amerika Nadeshiko: Japanese
     Immigrant Women in the United States, 1900-1924,"
     Pacific Historical Review, Vol. 49 (May 1980),
     pp. 339-357

263. Johnson, Dorothy E. "Organized Women as
     Lobbyists in the 1920's," Capital Studies, Vol. 1
     (Spring 1972), pp. 41-58

264. Katz, Jonathan, ed. Gay American History (New
     York: Avon Books, 1976)

265. Kelley, Mary, ed. Woman's Being, Woman's Place:
     Female Identity and Vocation in American History
     (Boston: G. K. Hall & Co., 1979)

266. Kennedy, David M. Birth Control in America: The
     Career of Margaret Sanger (New Haven, CT: Yale
     University Press, 1970)

30 AMERICAN WOMEN AND POLITICS

267. Kerber, Linda K. The Limits of Politicization: American Women and the American Revolution (Iowa City, IA: University of Iowa Press, 1982)

268. Kessler-Harris, Alice. Out to Work: A History of Wage Earning Women in the United States (New York: Oxford University Press, 1982)

269. Kessler-Harris, Alice. "Women's Wage Work as Myth and History," Labor History, Vol. 19 (Spring 1978), pp. 287-307

270. Klein, Viola. "The Historical Background," Women: A Feminist Perspective, Freeman, Jo, ed. (Palo Alto, CA: Mayfield, 1975), pp. 419-435

271. Kraditor, Aileen S. The Ideas of the Women's Suffrage Movement: 1880-1920 (New York: Columbia University Press, 1965)

272. Landers, E. M. "Effect of State Maximum-Hours Laws on the Employment of Women in 1920," Journal of Political Economy, Vol. 88 (June 1980), pp. 476-494

273. Lansing, Marjorie. "Political Change for the American Woman," Women in the World, Iglitzin, Lynne B. and Ruth Ross, eds. (Santa Barbara, CA: American Bibliographic Center Clio Press, 1976)

274. Laurentsen, John and David Thorstad. The Early Homosexual Rights Movement (1864-1935) (Albion, CA: Times Change Press, 1974)

275. Lerner, Gerda, ed. Black Women in White America: A Documentary History (New York: Vintage, 1973)

276. Lerner, Gerda. The Majority Finds its Past: Placing Women in History (Oxford: Oxford University Press, 1979)

277. Lines, Amelia Akehurst. To Raise Myself a Little: The Diaries and Letters of Jennie, a

Georgia Teacher, 1851-1886, Dyer, Thomas, ed.
(Athens, GA: University of Georgia Press, 1981,
c. 1947)

278. Longavex y Vasquez, Enriqueta. "The Mexican-
American Woman," Sisterhood is Powerful, Robin
Morgan, ed. (New York: Random House, 1970), pp.
379-384

279. Lunardini, C. A. and T. J. Knock. "Woodrow
Wilson and Woman Suffrage: A New Look,"
Political Science Quarterly, Vol. 95 (Winter
1980-1981), pp. 655-671

280. Marsh, Margaret S. "The Anarchist-Feminist
Response to the 'Woman Question' in Late
Nineteenth-Century America," American Quarterly,
Vol. 30 (Fall 1978), pp. 353-347

281. Mason, Karen Oppenheimer; John L. Czajka; and
Sara Arber. "Change in U.S. Women's Sex Role
Attitudes, 1964-1974," American Sociological
Review, Vol. 41 (August 1976), pp. 573-596

282. Mason, Mary Grimley and Carol Hurd Green, eds.
Journeys: Autobiographical Writings by Women
(Boston: G. K. Hall & Co., 1979)

283. Matthaei, Julie A. An Economic History of Women
in America: Women's Work, the Sexual Division of
Labor and the Development of Capitalism (New
York: Schocken Books, 1982)

284. Milkman, Ruth. "Organizing the Sexual Division of
Labor: Historical Perspectives on 'Women's Work'
and the American Labor Movement," Socialist
Review, Vol. 10, (January-February 1980), pp.
95-150

285. Morgan, Robin, ed. Sisterhood is Powerful (New
York: Random House, 1970)

286. O'Neill, William L. Everyone Was Brave: A
     History of Feminism in America (Chicago:
     Quadrangle Books, 1969)

287. Painter, Diann Holland. "The Black Woman in
     American History," Current History, Vol. 70 (May
     1976), pp. 224-228, p. 234

288. Papachristou, Judith. Women Together: A History
     in Documents of the Women's Movement in the
     United States (New York: Knopf, 1976)

289. Perdue, Theda, comp. Nations Remembered: An
     Oral History of the Five Civilized Tribes,
     1865-1907 (Westport, CT: Greenwood Press, 1980)

290. Porter, Jack N. "Rosa Sonnenschein and The
     American Jewess: The First Independent English
     Language Women's Journal in the United States,"
     American Jewish History, Vol. 68 (Summer 1978),
     pp. 57-63

291. Porter, Kirk Herald. A History of Suffrage in
     the United States (Westport, CT: Greenwood
     Press, 1969), reprint of 1918 edition

292. Rogge, John O. "Equal Rights for Women
     (Historical Analysis of the Body of Litigation
     Involving the Rights of Women)," Howard Law
     Journal Vol. 21 (November 2, 1978), pp. 327-420

293. Rothman, Sheila M. Woman's Proper Place (New
     York: Basic Books, 1978)

294. Rowbotham, Sheila. Hidden from History:
     Rediscovering Women in History from the 17th
     Century to the Present (New York: A Vintage
     Book, 1982)

295. Rowbotham, Sheila. Hidden from History: 300
     Years of Women's Oppression and the Fight
     Against It (London: Pluto Press, 1973)

296. Salper, Roberta, ed. Female Liberation: History
     and Current Politics (New York: Knopf, 1972)

297. Scharf, Lois. To Work and to Wed: Female
     Employment, Feminism, and the Great Depression
     (Westport, CT: Greenwood Press, 1980)

298. Schlissel, Lillian. Women's Diaries of the
     Westward Journey (New York: Schocken Books,
     1982)

299. Schneir, Miriam, ed. Feminism: The Essential
     Historical Writings (New York: A Vintage Book,
     1982)

300. Schramm, Sarah Slavin. Plow Women Rather Than
     Reapers: An Intellectual History of Feminism in
     the United States (Metuchen, NJ: Scarecrow
     Press, 1979)

301. Scott, Anne Firor. The Southern Lady: From
     Pedestal to Politics, 1830-1930 (Chicago:
     University of Chicago Press, 1972)

302. Shorter, Edward. The Making of the Modern Family
     (New York: Basic Books, 1975)

303. Sinclair, Andrew. The Better Half: The
     Emancipation of the American Woman (New York:
     Greenwood Press, 1965)

304. Small, S. E. "Yankee Schoolmarm in Freedman's
     Schools: An Analysis of Attitudes," Journal of
     Southern History, Vol. 45 (August 1979), pp.
     381-402

305. Strauss, Sylvia. Traitors to the Masculine
     Cause: The Men's Campaigns for Women's Rights
     (Westport, CT: Greenwood Press, 1982)

306. Sutherland, Elizabeth. "The Colonized Woman:
     The Chicana," Sisterhood is Powerful,

Morgan, Robin, ed. (New York: Random House, 1970), pp. 376-379

307. Tax, Meredith. The Rising of the Women: Feminist Solidarity and Class Conflict, 1880-1917 (New York: Monthly Review Press, 1981)

308. Ware, Susan. Beyond Suffrage: Women in the New Deal (Cambridge, MA: Harvard University Press, 1981)

309. Wertheimer, Barbara Meyer. We Were There: The Story of Working Women in America (New York: Pantheon Book, Inc., 1977)

310. Wiley, Bell Irvin. Confederate Women (Westport, CT: Greenwood Press, 1974)

311. Wilson, Margaret Gibbons. The American Woman in Transition: The Urban Influence, 1870-1920 (Westport, CT: Greenwood Press, 1979)

312. Withey, Lynne. Dearest Friend: A Life of Abigail Adams (New York: The Free Press, 1981)

313. "Women in America," Symposium, Current History, Vol. 7 (May 1976), pp. 193-234

314. Young, Louise M. "Women's Place in American Politics: The Historical Perspective," Journal of Politics, Vol. 38 (August 1976), pp. 295-346

III. THE NATURE-VERSUS-NURTURE DEBATE: Cultural and
Biological Antecedents of Behavior

315. Arms, Suzanne. Immaculate Deception: A New
Look at Childbirth in America (New York: Bantam
Books, 1975)

316. Bardwick, Judith M. Psychology of Women: A
Study of Bio-Cultural Conflicts (New York:
Harper & Row, 1971)

317. Bardwick, Judith M.; Elizabeth Douvan; Matina S.
Horner; and David Gutman. Feminine Personality
and Conflict (Belmont, CA: Greenwood Press,
1970)

318. Barlow, George W. and James Silverburg, eds.
Sociobiology: Beyond Nature-Nurture (Boulder,
CO: Westview, 1980)

319. Belotti, Elena Gianini. What are Little Girls
Made Of? The Roots of Feminine Stereotypes (New
York: Schocken Books, 1977)

320. Brabender, Virginia and Susan K. Boardman. "Sex
Differences in Self-Confidence as a Function of
Feedback and Social Cues," Psychological
Reports, Vol. 41 (December 1977), pp. 1007-1010

321. Braverman, I. K., et al. "Sex Role Stereotypes:
A Current Appraisal," The Journal of Social
Issues, Vol. 28, No. 2 (1972), pp. 59-78

322. Burnham, Dorothy. "Biology and Gender: False
     Theories about Women and Blacks," Freedomways,
     Vol. 17, No. 1 (1977), pp. 8-13

323. Caplan, Arthur L., ed. The Sociobiology Debate
     (New York: Harper and Row, 1978)

324. Chafetz, Janet S. Masculine, Feminine, or
     Human? An Overview of the Sociology of Sex
     Roles (Itasca, IL: F. E. Peacock Publishers,
     1978), particularly "Is Biology Destiny?" pp.
     1-32

325. Cherry, Frances and Kay Deaux. "Fear of Success
     Versus Fear of Gender-Inappropriate Behavior,"
     Sex Roles, Vol. 4 (Fall 1978), pp. 97-102

326. Chodorow, Nancy. "Considerations on a Biosocial
     Perspective on Parenting," Berkeley Journal of
     Sociology, Vol. 22, No. 22 (1977-78), pp.
     179-197

327. Chodorow, Nancy. "Family Structure and Feminine
     Personality," Woman Culture and Society,
     Rosaldo, Michelle Z. and Louise Lamphere, eds.
     (Stanford, CA: Stanford University Press,
     1974), pp. 43-66

328. Chodorow, Nancy. The Reproduction of Mothering:
     Psychoanalysis and the Sociology of Gender
     (Berkeley, CA: University of California Press,
     1978)

329. Davis, Enid. The Liberty Cap: A Catalogue of
     Non-Sexist Materials for Children (Chicago:
     Academy Chicago, 1978)

330. Deckard, Barbara Sinclair. "The Nature of
     Woman: Psychological Theories," in her The
     Women's Movement (New York: Harper & Row,
     1979), pp. 13-28

331. Dill, Bonnie Thorton. "The Dialectics of Black Womanhood," Signs, Vol. 4 (Spring 1979), pp. 543-555

332. Duffin, Lorna. "Prisoners of Progress: Women and Evolution," The Nineteenth Century Woman: Her Cultural and Physical World, Delamont, Sara and Lorna Duffin, eds. (New York: Barnes & Noble, 1978), pp. 57-91

333. Fletcher, Ronald. Sociobiology: The Study of Social Systems (New York: Scribner, 1981)

334. Francoeur, R. T. "Sexual Revolution: Will Hard Times Turn Back the Clock?" Futurist, Vol. 14 (April 1980), pp. 3-12

335. Frieze, Irene et al. Women and Sex Roles: A Social Psychological Perspective (New York: Norton & Co., 1978)

336. Freud, Sigmund. "Lectures on Femininity," "Moses and Monotheism," "Totem and Taboo," "The Case of Dora," Introductory Lectures on Psychoanalysis, Strachey, James, ed. and trans. (New York: W. W. Norton, 1977)

337. Gallop, Jane. The Daughter's Seduction: Feminism and Psychoanalysis (Ithaca, NY: Cornell University Press, 1982)

338. Gilder, George. Wealth and Poverty (New York: Basic Books, 1981)

339. Gilligan, Carol. In a Different Voice: Psychological Theory and Women's Development (Cambridge, MA: Harvard University Press, 1982)

340. Gilligan, Carol. "Woman's Place in Man's Life Cycle," Harvard Educational Review, Vol. 49 (November 1979), pp. 431-447

341. Goldberg, Steven. The Inevitability of
     Patriarchy (London: Temple Smith, 1977, revised
     edition)

342. Gough, Kathleen. "The Origin of the Family,"
     Toward an Anthropology of Women, Reiter, Rayna
     R., ed. (New York: Monthly Review Press, 1975),
     pp. 51-57

343. Gould, Stephen Jay. The Mismeasure of Man (about
     racism and sexism in IQ testing) (New York:
     Norton, 1981)

344. Gove, Walter and G. Russell Carpenter, eds. The
     Fundamental Connection Between Nature and
     Nurture (Lexington, MA: Lexington Books, 1981)

345. Gove, W. R. and M. Hughes. "Possible Causes of
     the Apparent Sex Differences in Physical Health:
     An Empirical Investigation," American
     Sociological Review, Vol. 44 (Fall 1979), pp.
     126-146; Discussion, Vol. 45 (June 1980), pp.
     507-522

346. Gross, Harriet Engel et al. "Considering a
     Biological Perspective on Parenting," Signs,
     Vol. 4 (Summer 1979), pp. 695-717

347. Gutmann, Amy. "Freud versus Feminism,"
     Dissent, Vol. 26 (Spring 1979), pp. 204-212

348. Hall, Diana Long. "Biology, Sex Hormones, and
     Sexism in the 1920s," Women and Philosophy,
     Gould, Carol and Mary Wartofsky, eds. (New
     York: G. P. Putnam's Sons, 1976)

349. Haraway, Donna. "Animal Sociology and a Natural
     Economy of the Body Politic," Signs, Vol. 4
     (Autumn 1978), pp. 21-60.

350. Harris, Dorothy V. "Physical Sex Differences:
     Being Male and Female in Sports Involvement,"

The Study of Women: Enlarging Perspectives of
Social Reality, Snyder, Eliose C., ed. (New
York: Harper & Row, 1979), pp. 184-206

351. Heilbrun, Carolyn G. Toward a Recognition of
Androgyny (New York: W. W. Norton and Co.,
1982)

352. Hrdy, Sarah B. The Woman That Never Evolved
(Cambridge, MA: Harvard University Press, 1981)

353. Hubbard, Ruth and Marian Lowe, eds. Genes and
Gender II (New York: Gordian Press, 1979)

354. Hunt, James, ed. Readings in Sociobiology (New
York: McGraw-Hill, 1980)

355. Jencks, Christopher et al. Inequality: A
Reassesment of the Effect of Family and
Schooling in America (New York: Harper and Row,
1973)

356. Lee, Patrick C. and Robert S. Stewart., eds. Sex
Differences: Cultural and Developmental
Dimensions (New York: Urizen Books, 1976)

357. LeGuin, Ursula. The Left Hand of Darkness (New
York: Ace Books, 1976)

358. Leibowitz, Leila. "Perspectives on the
Evolution of Sex Differences," Toward an
Anthropology of Women, Reiter, Rayna R., ed.
(New York: Monthly Review Press, 1975), pp.
20-35

359. Levine, Ellen and Judith Hole. "Biological
Differences Argument," Rebirth of Feminism,
Hole, Judith and Ellen Levine (New York:
Quadrangle Books, Inc., 1971), pp. 171-193

360. Lewontin, R. C. "Sociobiology as an Adaptionist
Program," Behavioral Science, Vol. 24 (January
1979), pp. 5-14

361. Lott, Bernice. Becoming a Woman (Springfield, MA: Charles C. Thomas, Publisher, 1981)

362. Lowe, Marian. "Sociobiology and Sex Differences," Signs, Vol. 4 (Autumn 1978), pp. 118-125

363. Lydon, S. "The Politics of Orgasm," Sisterhood is Powerful, Morgan, Robin, ed. (New York: Vintage, 1970), pp. 219-228

364. Maccoby, Eleanor E. and Carol N. Jacklin. "Myth, Reality, and Shades of Grey: What We Know and Don't Know About Sex Differences," Psychology Today, Vol. 8 (December 1974), pp. 109-112

365. May, Robert. Sex and Fantasy: Patterns of Male and Female Development (New York: W. W. Norton and Co., 1982)

366. Mead, Margaret. Male and Female (New York: William Morrow, 1949)

367. Mednick, Martha T. S.; Sandra S. Tangri; and Lois W. Hoffman, eds. Women and Achievement: Social and Motivational Analyses (New York: Halsted Press, 1975)

368. Mitchell, Juliet. Psychoanalysis and Feminism: Freud, Reich, Laing, and Women (New York: A Vintage Book, 1975)

369. Mitscherlich-Nielson, M. "Psychoanalysis and Female Sexuality," Partisan Review, Vol. 46, No. 1 (1979), pp. 61-74

370. Ortner, Sherry B. "Is Female to Male as Nature is to Culture?" Woman, Culture, and Society, Rosaldo, Michelle Z. and Louise Lamphere, eds. (Stanford, CA: Stanford University Press, 1974), pp. 67-87

371. Paige, Karen Eriksen and Jeffery M. Paige. The
     Politics of Reproductive Ritual (Berkeley, CA:
     University of California Press, 1981)

372. Reeves, Nancy. Womankind: Beyond the
     Stereotypes, (New York: Aldine Publishing Co.,
     1982, second edition)

373. Reiter, Rayna R., ed. Toward an Anthropology of
     Women (New York: Monthly Review Press, 1975)

374. Rogers, Susan Carol. "Woman's Place: A
     Critical Review of Anthropological Theory,"
     Comparative Studies in Society and History, Vol.
     20 (January 1978), pp. 123-162

375. Rosaldo, Michelle Z. and Louise Lamphere, eds.
     Woman, Culture, and Society (Stanford, CA:
     Stanford University Press, 1974)

376. Rossi, Alice S. "A Biological Perspective on
     Parenting," Daedalus, Vol. 106 (Spring 1977),
     pp. 1-32

377. Rubin, Gayle. "The Traffic in Women: Notes on
     the 'Political Economy of Sex'" Toward An
     Anthropology of Women, Reiter, Rayna, ed. (New
     York: Monthly Review Press, 1975)

378. Scarf, Maggie. "He and She: Sex Hormones and
     Behavior," in her Body, Mind, Behavior
     (Washington, DC: The New Republic Book Company,
     1976), pp. 19-35

379. Seward, John P. and Georgene H. Seward. Sex
     Differences: Mental and Temperamental
     (Lexington, MA: Lexington Books, 1980)

380. Sherif, Carolyn Wood. "What Every Intelligent
     Person Should Know About Psychology and Women,"
     The Study of Women: Enlarging Perspectives on
     Social Reality, Snyder, Eloise C., ed. (New
     York: Harper and Row, 1979), pp. 143-183

381. Skolnick, Arlene. The Intimate Environment:
     Exploring Marriage and the Family (Boston:
     Little, Brown, and Co., 1973), pp. 150-192

382. Tanner, Nancy and Adrienne Zihlman. "Women in
     Evolution, Part 1: Innovation and Selection in
     Human Origins," Signs, Vol. 1 (Spring 1976), pp.
     585-608

383. Terman, Lewis M. "Psychological Sex
     Differences," Manual of Child Psychology,
     Carmichael, Leonard, ed. (New York: Wiley,
     1954), pp. 954-1000

384. Thomas, L. "Sexism and Racism: Some Conceptual
     Differences," Ethics, Vol. 90 (January 1980),
     pp. 239-256

385. Tooney, Nancy. "The 'Math Gene' and Other
     Symptons of the Biology Backlash," Ms., Vol. 10
     (September 1981), pp. 56ff

386. "Toward a Feminist Theory of Motherhood,"
     Feminist Studies, Vol. 4 (June 1978), Special
     Issue

387. Unger, R. K. "Toward a Redefinition of Sex and
     Gender," American Psychology, Vol. 34 (November
     1979), pp. 1085-1094; Discussion, Vol. 35
     (October 1980), pp. 940-942

388. Vaughn, B. E. et al. "Relationship Between
     Out-of-Home Care and the Quality of
     Infant-Mother Attachment in an Economically
     Disadvantaged Population," Child Development,
     Vol. 51 (December 1980), pp. 1203-1214

389. Weisstein, Naomi. "Kinde, Kuche, Kirche as
     Scientific Law: Psychology Constructs the
     Female," Sisterhood is Powerful, Morgan, Robin,
     ed. (New York: Vintage, 1970), pp. 228-245

390. Weitz, Shirley. Sex Roles: Biological, Psychological, and Social Foundations (New York: Oxford University Press, 1977)

391. Williams, Juanita H. Psychology of Women: Behavior in a Biosocial Context (New York: W. W. Norton, 1974)

392. Wilson, Edward O. Sociobiology: The Abridged Edition (Cambridge, MA: Harvard University Press, 1980)

IV. WOMEN IN THE FAMILY: Power, Privilege, and
Responsibility

393. Aiken, William and Hugh LaFollette, eds. Whose
Child? Children's Rights, Parental Authority,
and State Power (Totowa, NJ: Rowman and
Littlefield, 1980)

394. Aries, Philippe. Centuries of Childhood: A
Social History of Family Life (New York: Random
House, 1965)

395. Baden, Clifford. Work and Family (Boston:
Wheelock College Center for Parenting Studies,
1981)

396. Bahr, Stephen J. "Effects on Power and Division
of Labor in Family," Working Mothers, Hoffman, L.
W. and F. I. Nye, eds. (San Francisco, CA:
Jossey-Bass, 1974), pp. 167-185

397. Bane, Mary Jo. Here to Stay: American Families
in the Twentieth Century (New York: Basic Books,
1976)

398. Basile, R.A. "Lesbian Mothers," Women's Rights
Law Reporter, Vol. 2 (December 1974), pp. 3-18

399. Becker, Gary S. A Treatise on the Family
(Cambridge, MA: Harvard University Press, 1981)

400. Beckman-Brindley, Sharon and Joseph B. Tavormina.
"Power Relationships in Families: A Social-

45

Exchange Perspective," Family Process, Vol. 17
(December 1978), pp. 423-436

401. Bell, Alan P. and Martin S. Weinberg. Homosexual
Ties: A Study of Diversity Among Men and Women
(New York: Simon and Schuster, 1978)

402. Bequaert, Lucia H. Single Women Alone and
Together (Boston: Beacon Press, Inc., 1976)

403. Bernard, Jessie S. The Future of Marriage (New
York: World, 1972)

404. Bernard, Jessie S. The Future of Motherhood (New
York: Dial Press, 1974)

405. Bernard, Jessie. Women, Wives, Mothers: Values
and Options (Chicago: Aldine, 1975)

406. Bianchi, Suzanne M. Household Composition and
Racial Inequality (New Brunswick, NJ: Rutgers
University Press, 1981)

407. "Black Families," Journal of Marriage and the
Family, Vol. 40 (November 1978), Special Issue

408. Bott, Elizabeth. Family and Social Network:
Rules, Norms and External Relationships in
Ordinary Urban Families (London: Tavistock,
1968)

409. Cates, Willard, Jr. "Legal Abortion: Are
American Black Women Healthier Because of It?",
Phylon, Vol. 38 (September 1977), pp. 267-281

410. Chapman, Jane Robert and Margaret Gates. Women
Into Wives: The Legal and Economic Impact of
Marriage (Beverly Hills, CA: Sage Publications,
Inc., 1977)

411. Chodorow, Nancy. The Reproduction of Mothering:
Psychoanalysis and the Sociology of Gender

(Berkeley, CA: University of California Press, 1978)

412. Cromwell, Ronald E. and David H. Olsen, eds. Power in Families (Beverly Hills, CA: Sage Publications, 1975)

413. Cronan, Sheila.   "Marriage," Radical Feminism, Koedt, Anne; Ellen Levine; and Anita Rapone, eds. (New York: Quadrangle, 1973), pp. 213-221

414. Davis, Margaret R.   Families in a Working World: The Impact of Organizations on the Domestic Life (New York: Praeger Publishers, 1982)

415. Deckard, Barbara.   "The Family: Refuge or Prison?" in her The Women's Movement (New York: Harper and Row, 1979) pp. 60-83

416. Dietrich, Katheryn Thomas.   "A Reexamination of the Myth of Black Patriarchy," Journal of Marriage and the Family, Vol. 37, No. 2 (May 1975), pp. 357-374

417. Dixon, Richard D.   "The 'Illegitimacy Runs in Families' Hypothesis is Reconsidered," Journal of Black Studies, Vol. 11 (March 1981), pp. 277-287

418. Eichler, Margrit.   "Power, Dependency, Love and the Sexual Division of Labour: A Critique of the Decision Making Approach to Family Power and an Alternative Approach with an Appendix: On Washing My Dirty Linen in Public," Women's Studies International Quarterly, Vol. 4, No. 2 (1981), pp. 201-219

419. Enloe, Cynthia.   "Women--The Reserve Army of Army Labor (Ideological Processes That Shape Three Spheres of Women's Military Use: As Soldiers, As Defense Industry Laborers, As Mothers of Future Soldiers)," Review of Radical Political Economy, Vol. 12 (Summer 1980), pp. 43-52

420. Foreman, Ann. Femininity as Alienation: Women
     and the Family in Marxism and Psychoanalysis
     (London: Pluto Press, 1977)

421. Fox, Bonnie, ed. Hidden in the Household:
     Women's Domestic Labour Under Capitalism
     (Toronto: Women's Educational Press, 1980)

422. Fraiberg, Selma. Every Child's Birthright: In
     Defense of Mothering (New York: Basic Books,
     1977)

423. Gerber, Gwendolyn R. and Joseph Balkin. "Sex
     Role Stereotypes as a Function of Marital Status
     and Role," The Journal of Psychology, Vol. 95
     (1977), pp. 9-16

424. Giele, Janet Zollinger. "Change in the Family
     Context," Women and the Future: Changing Sex
     Roles in Modern America (New York: The Free
     Press, 1978), pp. 188-242

425. Gilder, George. Wealth and Poverty (New York:
     Basic Books, 1981)

426. Gillespie, Dair L. "Who Has the Power: The
     Marital Struggle," Women: A Feminist
     Perspective, Freeman, Jo, ed. (Palo Alto, CA:
     Mayfield, 1975), pp. 64-88

427. Glazer-Malbin, Nona, ed. Old Family/New Family
     (New York: Van Nostrand Reinhold Co., 1975)

428. Gough, Kathleen. "The Origin of the Family,"
     Women: A Feminist Perspective, Freeman, Jo, ed.
     (Palo Alto, CA: Mayfield, 1975),
     pp. 43-64

429. Grossman, Allyson Sherman. "Working Mothers and
     Their Children," Monthly Labor Review, Vol. 104
     (May 1981), pp. 49-54

430. Gutman, Herbert G. The Black Family in Slavery and Freedom, 1750-1925 (New York: Random House, 1977)

431. Hanson, W. "Urban Indian Woman and Her Family," Social Casework, Vol. 61 (October 1980), pp. 476-483

432. Harding, Susan. "Family Reform Movements: Recent Feminism and its Oppositions," Feminist Studies, Vol. 7 (Spring 1981), pp. 57-75

433. Harrison, James B. "Men's Roles and Men's Lives," Signs, Vol. 4 (Winter 1978), pp. 324-336

434. Hartmann, Heidi I. "Family as the Locus of Gender, Class, and Political Struggle: The Example of Housework," Signs, Vol. 6 (Spring 1981), pp. 366-394

435. Henley, Nancy and Jo Freeman. "The Sexual Politics of Interpersonal Behavior," Women: A Feminist Perspective, Freeman, Jo, ed. (Palo Alto, CA: Mayfield, 1975), pp. 391-401

436. Hofferth, Sandra L. "Day Care in the Next Decade: 1980-1990," Journal of Marriage and the Family, Vol. 41 (August 1979), pp. 649-658

437. Hoffman, Lois W. "Parental Power Relations and the Division of Household Tasks," The Employed Mother in America, Nye, F. I. and L. W. Hoffman, eds. (Chicago: Rand McNally, 1963), pp. 215-230

438. Holstrom, Nancy. "'Women's Work,' the Family and Capitalism," Science and Society, Vol. 45 (Summer 1981), pp. 186-211

439. Husby, Ralph D. "Day Care for Families on Public Assistance: Workfare Versus Welfare," Industrial and Labor Relations Review, Vol. 27 (July 1974), pp. 503-510

440. Iglehart, Alfreda P. "Wives, Work, and Social
     Change: What About the Housewives?" Social
     Service Review, Vol. 54 (September 1980), pp.
     317-330

441. Johnson, Beverly L. "Women Who Head Families,
     1970-1977: Their Numbers Rose, Income Lagged:
     Since 1970, about 60% of the Increase Has Been
     Among Divorcees; The Income of One-Third of the
     Families Headed by Women Remains Below the
     Poverty Level," Monthly Labor Review, Vol. 101
     (February 1978), pp. 32-37

442. Jones, Elise F. "The Impact of Women's
     Employment on Marital Fertility in the U.S.
     1970-75," Population Studies, Vol. 35 (July
     1981), pp. 161-173

443. Kamerman, Sheila B. and Alfred J. Kahn. Child
     Care, Family Benefits, and Working Parents: A
     Study in Comparative Policy (New York: Columbia
     University Press, 1981)

444. Kamerman, Sheila B. and Alfred J. Kahn. Family
     Policy: Government and Families in Fourteen
     Countries (New York: Columbia University Press,
     1978)

445. Keller, Suzanne, ed. Building for Women
     (Lexington, MA: Lexington Books, 1981)

446. "The Labor of Women: Work and Family," Signs,
     Vol. 4 (Summer 1979), Special Issue

447. "Large Families Falling From Favor Here as Well
     as Abroad," Gallup Opinion Index (May 1974), pp.
     25-28

448. Lenero-Otero, Luis, ed. Beyond the Nuclear Family
     Model: Cross-Cultural Perspectives (Beverly
     Hills, CA: Sage, 1977)

449. Levine, James A. et al. for the United States
     Commission on Civil Rights. Child Care and Equal

Opportunity for Women (Washington, DC: U.S.
Government Printing Office, June 1981)

450. Levitan, Sar. What's Happening to the American
Family? (Baltimore, MD: Johns Hopkins
University Press, 1981)

451. Lopata, H. Z. "Contributions of Extended
Families to the Support Systems of Metropolitan
Area Widows: Limitations of the Modified Kin
Network," Journal of Marriage and Family, Vol. 40
(May 1978), pp. 355-364

452. MacDonald, M. and I. V. Sawhill. "Welfare Policy
and the Family," Public Policy, Vol. 26 (Winter
1978), pp. 89-119

453. Mack, Delores E. "The Power Relationship in
Black Families and White Families," Journal of
Personality and Social Psychology, Vol. 30
(Summer, 1974), pp. 409-413

454. Modell, J. "Suburbanization and Change in the
American Family," Journal of Interdisciplinary
History, Vol. 9 (Spring 1979), pp. 621-646

455. Morgan, James N. et al. Five Thousand American
Families--Patterns of Economic Progress, Vols.
1-9 (Ann Arbor, MI: Survey Research Center,
Institute for Social Research, University of
Michigan, Vol. 1, 1974; Vol. 9, 1981)

456. "The Motherhood Mandate," Psychology of Women
Quarterly, Vol. 4 (Fall 1979). Special issue
deals with sex roles, labor force participation,
fertility, attitudes toward motherhood

457. Mott, Frank L. with Steven H. Sandell; David
Schapiro; Patricia K. Brito; Timothy J. Carr;
Carol Jusenius; Peter J. Koenig; and Sylvia F.
Moore, Center for Human Resource Research, The
Ohio State University. Women, Work, and Family:

Dimensions of Change in American Society
(Lexington, MA: Lexington Books, 1978)

458. Nye, Francis Ivan and Lois Wladis Hoffman, eds.
The Employed Mother in America (Westport, CT:
Greenwood Press, 1976) reprint of 1963 edition

459. Oakley, Ann. The Sociology of Housework (New
York: Pantheon Books, 1974)

460. Oppenheimer, Valerie Kincade. "The Sociology of
Women's Economic Role in the Family," American
Sociological Review, Vol. 42 (June 1977), pp.
387-406

461. Outhwaite. R. B. "Population Change, Family
Structure and the Good of Counting; Review
Article," History Journal, Vol. 22 (March 1979),
pp. 229-237

462. Packer, Arnold H. "Birth Planning Success:
Motivation and Contraceptive Method," Family
Planning Perspectives, Vol. 10 (January-February
1978), pp. 43-48

463. Peplau, L. A. et al. "Loving Women: Attachment
and Autonomy in Lesbian Relationships," Journal
of Social Issues, Vol. 34, No. 3 (1978), pp. 7-27

464. Petchesky, Rosalind Pollack. "Antiabortion,
Antifeminism, and the Rise of the New Right,"
Feminist Studies, Vol. 7 (Summer 1981), pp.
206-246

465. Rapoport, Rhona; Robert N. Rapoport; and Janice
Burnstead. Working Couples (New York: Harper &
Row, 1978)

466. Rapoport, Rhona; Robert N. Rapoport; and Zoni
Strelitz (with Stephen Kew). Fathers, Mothers
and Society: Toward New Alliances (New York:
Basic Books, 1977)

467. "Reason Interview: Thomas Sowell; A UCLA
     (University of California at Los Angeles)
     Economist Talks About Blacks and the Marketplace,
     Women and Work, Freedom and Equality," Reason,
     Vol. 12 (December 1980), pp. 44-51

468. Rich, Adrienne. Of Woman Born: Motherhood as
     Experience and Institution (New York: Norton,
     1976)

469. Ross, Heather L. and Isabel V. Sawhill. "Families
     Headed by Women: Their Growth and Changing
     Composition," "Marital Instability," "Race and
     Family Structure," "What Happens to Children in
     Female-Headed Families?" Time of Transition: The
     Growth of Families Headed by Women (Washington,
     DC: Urban Institute, 1975), pp. 9-93, 129-153

470. Rothman, Barbara Katz. In Labor: Women and
     Power in the Birthplace (New York: Norton
     Publishers, 1982)

471. Safilos-Rothschild, Constantina. Love, Sex, and
     Sex Roles (Englewood Cliffs, NJ: Prentice-Hall,
     1977)

472. Scanzoni, John. Sex Roles, Women's Work, and
     Marital Conflict: A Study of Family Change
     (Lexington, MA: D.C. Heath & Co., 1978)

473. Schorr, Alvin L. "Single Parents, Women, and
     Public Policy," Institute of Socioeconomic
     Studies Journal, Vol. 6 (Winter 1981-1982), pp.
     100-113

474. Shorter, Edward. The Making of the Modern Family
     (New York: Basic Books, 1975)

475. Skolnick, Arlene. The Intimate Environment:
     Exploring Marriage and the Family (Boston:
     Little Brown and Co., 1973)

476. Skolnick, Arlene S. and Jerome H. Skolnick.
     Family in Transition: Rethinking Marriage,
     Sexuality, Child-Rearing, and Family Organization
     (Boston: Little, Brown, 1977, second edition)

477. Smith, Audrey D. and William J. Reid. "Child
     Care Arrangements of AFDC Mothers in the Work
     Incentive Program," Child Welfare, Vol. 52
     (December 1973), pp. 651-661

478. Sokoloff, Natalie J. Between Money and Love:
     The Dialectics of Women's Home and Market Work
     (New York: Praeger Publishers, 1980)

479. Staples, Robert, ed. The Black Family: Essays
     and Studies (Belmont, CA: Wadsworth Publishing,
     1971)

480. Staples, Robert. The Black Woman in America:
     Sex, Marriage, and the Family (Chicago:
     Nelson-Hall Publishers, 1973)

481. Staples, Robert. "Myths of Black Macho: A
     Response to Angry Black Feminists," Black
     Scholar, Vol. 10 (March-April 1979), pp. 24-36

482. Steinem, Gloria. "In the Middle of the Backlash:
     Some Cheerful Words About Men," Ms., Vol. 9 (June
     1981), p. 43ff

483. Steiner, Gilbert Y. The Futility of Family
     Policy (Washington, DC: The Brookings
     Institution, 1981)

484. Stencel, Sandra. "The Changing American Family,"
     Editorial Research Reports, Vol. I (June 3,
     1977), pp. 415-32

485. Stencel, Sandra. "Single Parent Families",
     Editorial Research Reports, Vol. II (September
     10, 1976), pp. 663-80

486. Stone, Lawrence. The Family, Sex and Marriage in
     England: 1500-1800 (New York: Harper & Row,
     1977)

487. Swerdlow, Amy, et al. Household and Kin:
     Families in Flux (Old Westbury, NY: Feminist
     Press, 1981)

488. Syfers, Judy. "Why I Want a Wife," Radical
     Feminism, Koedt, Anne; Ellen Levine; and Anita
     Rapone, eds. (New York: Quadrangle, 1973), pp.
     60-62

489. Tanner, Donna M. The Lesbian Couple (Lexington,
     MA: Lexington Books, 1978)

490. Thorne, Barrie and Marilyn Yalom, eds.
     Rethinking the Family: Some Feminist Questions
     (New York: Longman, 1982)

491. Tilly, Louise A. "The Family and Change," Theory
     and Society, Vol. 5 (May 1978), pp. 421-434

492. Tilly, Louise A. and Joan W. Scott. Women, Work
     and Family (New York: Holt, Rinehart and Wilson,
     1978)

493. "Toward a Feminist Theory of Motherhood,"
     Feminist Studies, Vol. 4 (June 1978), Special
     Issue

494. Tufte, Virginia, and Barbara Myerhoff, eds.
     Changing Images of the Family: Multidisciplinary
     Perspectives (New Haven, CT: Yale University
     Press, 1979)

495. United States Department of Health, Education and
     Welfare. Child Care and the Working Woman:
     Report and Recommendations of the Secretary's
     Advisory Committee on the Rights and
     Responsibilities of Women, 1975 (Washington, DC:
     U.S. Government Printing Office, 1976)

496. United States Social Security Administration,
     Office of Policy, Office of Research and
     Statistics."--Thy Father and Thy Mother--": A
     Second Look at Filial Responsibility and Family

Policy; A Reevaluation of Current Practice of
Filial Responsibility in the United States Two
Decades Later and its Relationship to the
Changing Social Security Programs (Washington,
DC: U.S. Government Printing Office, July 1980)

497. Vickery, Clair, et al. "Unemployment Rate Targets
and Anti-Inflation Policy as More Women Enter the
Workforce [with discussion]." American Economic
Review, Papers and Proceedings, Vol. 68 (May
1978), pp. 90-98

498. Vickery, Clair. "Women's Economic Contribution to
the Family," The Subtle Revolution: Women at
Work, Smith, Ralph E., ed. (Washington, DC: The
Urban Institute, 1979), pp. 159-201

499. Vida, Ginny, ed. Our Right to Love: A Lesbian
Resource Book (New York: Prentice-Hall, 1978)

500. Waite, Linda J. "Changes in Child Care
Arrangments of Working Women from 1965 to 1971,"
Social Science Quarterly, Vol. 58 (September
1977), pp. 302-311

501. Wallace, Michele. Black Macho and the Myth of
Superwoman (New York: Dial, 1979)

502. Warrior, Betsy. "Housework: Slavery or Labor of
Love?" Radical Feminism, Koedt Anne; Ellen
Levine; and Anita Rapone, eds. (New York:
Quadrangle, 1973), pp. 208-212

503. Wattenberg, Esther. "Female-Headed Families:
Trends and Implications," Social Work, Vol. 24
(November 1979), pp. 460-467

504. Weitzman, Lenore J. The Marriage Contract:
Spouses, Lovers, and the Law (New York: The Free
Press, 1980)

505. Wolf, Deborah Goleman. The Lesbian Community
     (Berkeley, CA: University of California Press,
     1979)

506. "Women, Class and the Family: Third Special
     Issue on the Political Economy of Women," Review
     of Radical Political Economy, Vol. 9 (Fall 1977),
     pp. 1-78

507. Worsnop, Richard. "Sexual Revolution: Myth or
     Reality," Editorial Research Reports, Vol. 1
     (April 1, 1970), pp. 239-258

508. Zaretsky, Eli. Capitalism, The Family and
     Personal Life (New York: Harper and Row, 1976)

V. POLITICAL SOCIALIZATION AND ATTITUDE FORMATION

509. Adell, Judith and Hilary Dole Klein. A Guide to Non-Sexist Children's Books (Chicago: Academy Chicago, 1976)

510. Allen, W. R. "Search for Applicable Theories of Black Family Life," Journal of Marriage and the Family, Vol. 40 (February 1978), pp. 117-129

511. Baruch, Rhoda. "The Achievement Motive in Women: Implications for Career Development," Journal of Personality and Social Psychology, Vol. 5 (February 1967), pp. 260-267

512. Bem, Sandra L. and Daryl J. Bem. "Case Study of a Nonconscious Ideology: Training the Woman to Know Her Place," Beliefs, Attitudes, and Human Affairs, Bem, Daryl J., ed. (Belmont, CA: Brooks Cole, 1970), pp. 89-100

513. "Black Families," Journal of Marriage and the Family, Vol. 40 (November 1978), Special Issue

514. "The Black Sexism Debate," Black Scholar, Vol. 10 (May-June 1979)

515. Bowker, Lee H. "Racism and Sexism: Hints Toward a Theory of the Causal Structure of Attitudes Toward Women," International Journal of Women's Studies, Vol. 4 (May-June 1981), pp. 277-288

516. Chafetz, Janet S. Masculine, Feminine or Human?
An Overview of the Sociology of Sex Roles
(Itasca, IL: F. E. Peacock Publishers, Inc.,
1978), particularly "The Bringing Up of Dick and
Jane," pp. 66-109

517. Clark, J. L. "Coming Out: The Process and Its
Price," Christianity and Crisis, Vol. 39 (June
11, 1979), pp. 149-153

518. deFord, Miriam Allen. "'Women Against
Themselves'; a sizeable proportion of articulate
American women honestly believe that they are
inferior [and] that the male should be dominant,"
Humanist, Vol. 31 (January-February 1971), pp.
8-9

519. Dworkin, R. J. "Ideology Formation: A Linear
Structural Model of Influences on Feminist
Ideology," Sociological Quarterly, Vol. 20
(Summer 1979), pp. 345-358

520. Feltner, Paula and Leneen Goldie. "Impact of
Socialization and Personality on the Female
Voter: Speculations Tested with 1964
Presidential Data," Western Political Quarterly,
Vol. 27 (December 1974), pp. 680-692

521. Feminists on Children's Media "A Feminist Look at
Children's Books," Radical Feminism, Koedt, Anne;
Ellen Levine; and Anita Rapone; eds. (New York:
Quadrangle, 1973), pp. 94-106

522. Flora, Cornelia B. and Naomi B. Lynn. "Women and
Political Socialization: Considerations of the
Impact of Motherhood," Women in Politics,
Jaquette, Jane S., ed. (New York: Wiley, 1974),
pp. 37-53

523. Fulenwider, Claire Knoche. Feminism in American
Politics: A Study of Ideological Influence (New
York: Praeger, 1980)

524. Gerber, Gwendolyn and Joseph Balkin. "Sex Role
     Stereotypes as a Function of Marital Status and
     Role," Journal of Psychology, Vol. 95 (1977), pp.
     9-16

525. Greenstein, Fred. "Sex-Related Political
     Differences in Childhood," Journal of Politics,
     Vol. 23 (May 1961), pp. 353-371

526. Halas, Celia M. "Sex Role Stereotypes:
     Perceived Childhood Socialization Experiences and
     the Attitudes and Behavior of Adult Women," The
     Journal of Psychology, Vol. 88 (November 1974),
     pp. 261-275

527. Hall, J. R. and J. D. Black. "Assertiveness,
     Aggressiveness and Attitudes Toward Feminism,"
     Journal of Social Psychology, Vol. 107 (February
     1979), pp. 57-62

528. Hershey, Marjorie R. "Racial Differences in
     Sex-Role Identities and Sex Stereotyping:
     Evidence Against a Common Assumption," Social
     Science Quarterly, Vol. 58 (March 1978), pp.
     583-596

529. Heiskanin, Veronica Stolte. "Sex Roles, Social
     Class, and Political Consciousness," Acta
     Sociologica, Vol. 14, Nos. 1-2 (1971), pp. 83-95

530. Hess, Robert and Judith Torney. The Development
     of Political Attitudes in Children (Chicago:
     Aldine Publishing Company, 1967)

531. Heyward, C. "Coming Out: Journey Without Maps,"
     Christianity and Crisis, Vol. 39 (June 11, 1979)
     pp. 153-156

532. Hoffman, Lois W. "Changes in Family Roles,
     Socialization, and Sex Differences," American
     Psychologist, Vol. 32, (August 1977), pp. 644-657

533. Holahan, Carole K. and Lucia A. Gilbert.
     "Conflict Between Major Life Role: Women and Men
     in Dual Career Couples," Human Relations, Vol. 32
     (June 1979), pp. 451-467

534. Holsti, Ole and James Rosenau. "The Foreign
     Policy Beliefs of Women in Leadership Positions,"
     Journal of Politics, Vol. 43 (May 1981), pp.
     326-347

535. Iglitzin, Lynne B. "The Making of the Apolitical
     Woman: Femininity and Sex-Stereotyping in
     Girls," Women in Politics, Jaquette, Jane S., ed.
     (New York: Wiley, 1974), pp. 25-37

536. Jennings, M. Kent and Kenneth P. Langton.
     "Mothers vs. Fathers: The Formation of Political
     Orientations Among Young Americans," Journal of
     Politics, Vol. 31 (May, 1969), pp. 329-357

537. Jennings, M. Kent and Richard G. Niemi.
     Generations and Politics: A Panel Study of Young
     Adults and their Parents (Princeton, NJ:
     Princeton University Press, 1981)

538. Jennings, M. Kent and Richard G. Niemi. The
     Political Character of Adolescence: The
     Influence of Families and Schools (Princeton, NJ:
     Princeton University Press, 1974)

539. Kaufman, Debra R. and Barbara L. Richardson.
     Achievement and Women: Challenging the
     Assumptions (New York: The Free Press, 1982)

540. Kundsin, Ruth B., ed. Women and Success: The
     Anatomy of Adhievement (New York: William Morrow
     & Co., 1974)

541. Laws, Judith Long. The Second X: Sex and Social
     Role (New York: Greenwood Press, 1979)

542. Murray, Pauli. "The Liberation of Black Women,"
Women: A Feminist Perspective, Freeman, Jo, ed.
(Palo Alto, CA: Mayfield, 1975), pp. 351-363

543. Nemerowicz, Gloria Morris. Children's
Perceptions of Gender and Work Roles (New York:
Praeger Publishers, 1979)

544. Orum, Anthony M.; Roberta S. Cohen; Sherri
Grasmuck; and Amy W. Orum. "Sex, Socialization,
and Politics," American Sociological Review, Vol.
39 (April 1974), pp. 197-209

545. Peek, Charles W. and S. Brown. "Sex Prejudice
Among White Protestants: Like or Unlike Ethnic
Prejudice," Social Forces, Vol. 59 (September
1980), pp. 169-185

546. Plax, Timothy G. and Lawrence B. Rosenfeld.
"Antecedents of Change in Attitudes of Males and
Females," Psychological Reports, Vol. 41, Part 1,
(December 1977), pp. 811-821

547. Ponse, Barbara. Identities in the Lesbian World:
The Social Construction of Self (Westport, CT:
Greenwood Press, 1978)

548. Rich, Adrienne. Of Woman Born (New York: Bantam
Books, Inc., 1976)

549. Sapiro, Virginia. "News From the Front:
Intersex and Intergenerational Conflict Over the
Status of Women," Western Political Quarterly,
Vol. 33 (June 1980), pp. 260-277

550. Sexism in Children's Books: Facts, Figures, and
Guidelines (London: Writers and Readers
Publishing Cooperative, 1976)

551. Sherman, S. J. "Attitude Bolstering When
Behavior is Inconsistent With Central Attitudes,"
Journal of Experimental Social Psychology, Vol.
16 (July 1980), pp. 388-403

552. Sigel, R. S. and J. V. Reynolds. "Generational
     Differences and the Women's Movement," Political
     Science Quarterly, Vol. 94, (Winter 1979-1980),
     pp. 635-648

553. Smith, M.D. and G.D. Self. "Feminists and
     Traditionalists: An Attitudinal Comparison," Sex
     Roles, Vol. 7 (February 1981), pp. 183-188

554. Smith, M. D. "Congruence Between Mothers and
     Daughters Sex-Role Attitudes: A Research Note,"
     Journal of Marriage and the Family, Vol. 42
     (February 1980), pp. 105-109

555. Steiger, J. C. "Influences of the Feminist
     Subculture in Changing Sex-Role Attitudes," Sex
     Roles, Vol. 7 (June 1981), pp. 627-633

556. Sutherland, Elyse. "Fear of Success and the Need
     for Power," Psychological Reports, Vol. 443
     (December 1978), pp. 763-766

557. Tedin, Kent L., et al. "Social Background and
     Political Differences Between Pro- and Anti-ERA
     Activists," American Politics Quarterly, Vol. 5
     (July 1977), pp. 395-408

558. Thornton, Arlan and Deborah Freedman. "Changes
     in the Sex Role Attitudes of Women, 1962-1977:
     Evidence From a Panel Study," American
     Sociological Review, Vol. 44 (October 1979), pp.
     831-843

559. Tuchman, Gaye, et al., eds. Health and Home:
     Images of Women in the Mass Media (Oxford:
     Oxford University Press, 1978)

560. Tyer, Z. E. and C. J. Erdwins. "Relationship of
     Sex Role to Male- and Female-Dominated
     Professions," Psychology Reporter, Vol. 44 (June
     1979), p. 1134

561. Walsh, M. Cay. "Attitudinal Measures and
     Evaluation of Males and Females in Leadership
     Roles," Psychological Reports, Vol. 45 (August
     1979), pp. 19-22

562. Weitzman, Lenore J. "Sex Role Socialization,"
     Women: A Feminist Perspective, Freeman, Jo, ed.
     (Palo Alto, CA: Mayfield, 1975), pp. 105-144

563. Weitzman, Lenore J. et al. "Sex Role
     Socialization in Picture Books for Preschool
     Children," American Journal of Sociology, Vol. 77
     (May 1972), pp. 1125-1150

564. White, M.C.; G. De Sanctis; and M.D. Crino.
     "Achievement, Self-Confidence, Personality Traits
     and Leadership Ability: A Review of Literature
     on Sex Differences," Psychological Reports, Vol.
     48 (April 1981), pp. 547-569

565. Zey-Ferrell, M. "Intergenerational Socialization
     of Sex-Role Attitudes: A Gender or Generation
     Gap?" Adolescence, Vol. 13 (Spring 1979), pp.
     95-108

VI. WOMEN AT WORK AND AT LEISURE

566. Agassi, Judith Buber. Women on the Job: The Attitudes of Women to Their Work (Lexington, MA: Lexington Books, 1979)

567. Almquist, Elizabeth McTaggart. Minorities, Gender and Work (Toronto: D.C. Heath Canada, Ltd., 1979)

568. Amsden, Alice, ed. The Economics of Women and Work (New York: St. Martin's Press, 1980)

569. Andre, Rae. Homemakers: The Forgotten Workers (Chicago: University of Chicago Press, 1981)

570. Antos, Joseph R. "Sex Differences in Union Membership," Industrial and Labor Relations Review, Vol. 33 (January 1980), pp. 162-169

571. Applebaum, Eileen. Back to Work: Determinants of Women's Successful Re-entry (Boston: Auburn House Publishing Co., 1981)

572. Arbogast, Kate A. "Women in the Armed Forces: A Rediscovered Resource," Military Review, Vol. 53 (November 1973), pp. 9-19

573. "As Men Move in On Women's Jobs: Some of Them Take 'Female' Jobs as Steppingstones; Many Like the Pay, Other Benefits; Result: Thousands of Men Entering Unisex Jobs," U.S. News, Vol. 91 (August 10, 1981), pp. 55-57

574. Aschenfelter, O. "Estimating the Effect of
     Training Programs on Earnings," Review of
     Economic Statistics, Vol. 60 (February 1978), pp.
     47-57

575. Baas, Bernard M.; Judith Krussell; and Ralph A.
     Alexander. "Male Managers' Attitudes Toward
     Working Women," American Behavioral Scientist,
     Vol. 15 (November-December 1971), pp. 221-236

576. Baden, Clifford. Work and Family (Boston:
     Wheelock College Center for Parenting Studies,
     1981)

577. Baer, Judith A. The Chains of Protection: The
     Judicial Response to Women's Labor Legislation
     (Westport, CT: Greenwood Press, 1978)

578. Baruch, Rhoda. "The Achievement Motive in Women:
     Implications for Career Development," Journal of
     Personality and Social Psychology, Vol. 5
     (February 1967), pp. 260-267

579. Baxandall, Rosalyn; Linda Gordon; and Susan
     Reverby, eds. America's Working Women: A
     Documentary History--1600 to the Present (New
     York: Vintage Books, 1976)

580. Bell, Duran. "Why Participation of Black and
     White Wives Differ," Journal of Human Resources,
     Vol. 9 (Fall 1974), pp. 465-479

581. Beller, A. H. "Effect of Economic Conditions on
     the Success of Equal Employment Opportunity Laws:
     An Application to the Sex Differential in
     Earnings," Review of Economics and Statistics,
     Vol. 62 (August 1980), pp. 379-387

582. Berch, Bettina. The Endless Day: The Political
     Economy of Women and Work (New York: Harcourt,
     Brace, Jovanovich, 1982)

583. Bergmann, B. R. and I. Adelman. "The Economic
     Role of Women," The American Economic Review,
     Vol. 63 (September 1973), pp. 509-514

584. Berquist, Virginia A. "Women's Participation in
     Labor Organizations: Expansion of Women's
     Participation in Labor Groups is Not Matched by
     an Increase in Leadership Positions," Monthly
     Labor Review, Vol. 97 (October 1974), pp. 3-9

585. Bianchi, S. M. "Racial Differences in Per Capita
     Income, 1960-76: The Importance of Household
     Size, Headship and Labor Force Participation,"
     Demography, Vol. 17 (May 1980), pp. 129-143

586. Bird, Caroline. The Two-Paycheck Marriage: How
     Women at Work are Changing Life in America: An
     In-Depth Report on the Great Revolution of Our
     Times (New York: Rawson, Wade Publications,
     1979)

587. Blau, Francine D. and Carol L. Jusenius.
     "Economists' Approach to Sex Segregation in the
     Labor Market: An Appraisal," Signs, Vol. 1,
     (Spring 1975), pp. 188-199

588. Blau, Francine D. and Lawrence M. Kahn. "Causes
     and Consequences of Layoffs (Comparison of
     Effects on Blacks, Whites and Women; U.S.),"
     Economic Inquiry, Vol. 19 (April 1981), pp.
     270-296

589. Blaxall, Martha and Barbara Reagan, eds. Women
     and the Workplace: The Implications of
     Occupational Segregation (Chicago: University of
     Chicago Press, 1976)

590. Bock, E. Wilbur. "The Case of the Negro Female
     Professionals," Phylon, Vol. 30 (Spring 1969),
     pp. 17-26

591. Bould, Sally. "Black and White Families:
     Factors Affecting the Wife's Contribution to the

Family Income Where the Husband's Income is Low to Moderate," The Sociological Quarterly, Vol. 18 (Autumn 1977), pp. 536-547

592. Bowers, Norman. "Have Employment Patterns in Recessions Changed? A Survey of Postwar Recessions Shows That the Increasing Proportion of Service Sector Jobs Has Moderated Overall Employment Declines; Women in Nontraditional Jobs, Blacks, and Youths Bear a Disproportionate Share of the Job Losses," Monthly Labor Review, Vol. 104 (February 1981), pp. 15-28

593. Brammer, Dana B. "A Look at Women Workers Today," Public Administration Survey, Vol. 25 (November 1977), pp. 1-4

594. Branca, Patricia. "A New Perspective on Women's Work: A Comparative Typology," Journal of Social History, Vol. 9 (June 1975), pp. 129-153

595. Bridges, William P. and Richard A. Birk. "Sex, Earnings, and the Nature of Work: A Job-Level Analysis of Male-Female Income Differences," Social Science Quarterly, Vol. 58 (March 1978), pp. 553-565

596. Brown, R. S. et al. "Incorporating Occupational Attainment in Studies of Male-Female Earnings Differentials," Journal of Human Resources, Vol. 15 (Winter 1980), pp. 3-28

597. Burstein, Paul. "Equal Employment Legislation and the Income of Women and Nonwhites," American Sociological Review, Vol. 44 (June 1979), pp. 367-391

598. Cahn, Ann Foote, ed. Women in the U. S. Labor Force (New York: Praeger Publishers, 1978)

599. Campbell, Helen Stuart. Prisoners of Poverty: Women Wage-Workers, Their Trades and Their Lives

(Westport, CT: Greenwood Press, 1972) reprint of 1887 edition

600. Cantor, Milton and Bruce Laurie, eds. Class, Sex and the Woman Worker (Westport, CT: Greenwood Press, 1977)

601. Carliner, G. "Female Labor Force Participation Rates for Nine Ethnic Groups," Journal of Human Resources, Vol. 16 (Spring 1981), pp. 286-293

602. Chenoweth, Lillian and Elizabeth Maret. "The Labor Force Patterns of Mature Rural Women (Age 30-44; United States)," Rural Sociology, Vol. 44 (Winter 1979), pp. 736-753

603. Chernow, Ron. "All in A Day's Work: Housekeepers, Mostly Black Women, Are The Last Frontier of Labor Organizing," Mother Jones, Vol. 1 (August 1976), pp. 11-16

604. Chiswick, Barry R. "Immigrant Earnings Patterns by Sex, Race, and Ethnic Groupings: Based On 1970 Census Data, Most Immigrant Men Reach Earnings Equality With the Native Born In 11-15 Years; For Women Earnings Following Arrival Vary More By Racial and Ethnic Group; Skills and Motive For Moving Affect Performance," Monthly Labor Review, Vol. 103 (October 1980), pp. 22-25

605. Corcoran, Mary and Greg J. Duncan. "Work History, Labor Force Attachment, and Earning Differences Between the Races and Sexes," The Journal of Human Resources, Vol. 14 (Winter 1979), pp. 3-20

606. Corcoran, Mary. "The Structure of Female Wages," American Economic Review, Vol. 68 (May 1978), pp. 165-170

607. Cramer, James C. "Employment Trends of Young Mothers and the Opportunity Cost of Babies in the

United States," Demography, Vol. 16 (May 1979),
pp. 177-197

608. Crothers, Diane. "The AT&T Settlement," Women's
Rights Law Reporter, Vol. 1 (Summer 1973), pp.
5-13

609. Danziger, Sheldon. "Do Working Wives Increase
Family Income Inequality?" (with a reply by B. R.
Bergmann and others), Journal of Human Resources,
Vol. 15 (Summer 1980) pp. 444-455

610. Davis, Joe C. and Carl M. Hubbard. "On the
Measurement of Discrimination Against Women,"
American Journal of Economics and Sociology, Vol.
38 (July 1979), pp. 287-290

611. Davis, Margaret R. Families in a Working World:
The Impact of Organizations on the Domestic Life
(New York: Praeger, 1982)

612. Deckard, Barbara. "The Self-Fulfilling Prophecy:
Sex Role Socialization," "The Exploitation of
Working Women," "The Professional Women: The
Obstacle Course," in her The Women's Movement
(New York: Harper & Row, 1979), pp. 29-59,
84-151

613. Dewey, Lucretia M. "Women in Labor Unions,"
Monthly Labor Review, Vol. 94 (February 9, 1971),
pp. 42-48

614. Donahue, Mary H. "The Female Labor Force in the
United States," The Geographical Record, Vol. 61
(July 1971), pp. 440-442

615. Duncan, Beverly. "Change in Worker/Nonworker
Ratios for Women (United States, 1948-1978),"
Demography, Vol. 16 (November 1979), pp. 535-547

616. Eisenstein, Zillah. Capitalist Patriarchy and
the Case for Socialist Feminism (New York:
Monthly Review Press, 1979)

617. Ellis, Judy Trent. "Sexual Harassment and Race: A Legal Analysis of Discrimination," Journal of Legislation, Vol. 8 (Winter 1981), pp. 30-45

618. England, Paula. "Women and Occupational Prestige: A Case of Vacuous Sex Equality," Signs, Vol. 5 (Winter 1979), pp. 252-265

619. Epstein, Cynthia F. Woman's Place: Options and Limits in Professional Careers (Berkeley, CA: University of California Press, 1970)

620. Epstein, Cynthia F. "Positive Effects of the Multiple Negative: Explaining the Success of Black Professional Women," American Journal of Sociology, Vol. 78 (January 1973), pp. 150-173

621. "Equal Pay, Comparable Work, and Job Evaluation," Yale Law Journal, Vol. 90 (January 1981), pp. 657-680

622. Featherman, David L. and Robert M. Houser. "Sexual Inequalities and Socio-Economic Achievement in the U.S., 1962-1973," American Sociological Review, Vol. 41 (June 1976), pp. 462-483

623. Feldberg, Roslyn L. and Evelyn Nakano Glenn. "Male and Female: Job Versus Gender Models in the Sociology of Work," Social Problems, Vol. 26 (June 1979), pp. 524-538

624. Ferber, Marianne and Helen Lowry. "Women--the New Reserve Army of the Unemployed," Signs, Vol. 1 (Spring 1976), pp. 213-232

625. Ferree, Myra M. "Working Class Feminism: A Consideration of the Consequences of Employment," Sociological Quarterly, Vol. 21 (Spring 1980), pp. 173-184

626. Ferree, Myra M. "Employment Without Liberation:
     Cuban Women in the United States," Social Science
     Quarterly, Vol. 60 (June 1979), pp. 35-50

627. Fierst, Edith U. "Why Congress Zapped Pensions
     for Women: A Half a Million Women Unknowingly
     Are Donating Their Tax-Deferred Pensions to Their
     More Affluent Bosses; When the Internal Revenue
     Service Tried to Do Something About It, Congress
     Said 'No'; Here's Why—and a Chance to Turn
     Congress Around," Graduate Woman, Vol. 75
     (November-December 1981), pp. 16-18

628. Finegan, T. Aldrich. "Participation of Married
     Women in the Labor Force," Sex, Discrimination,
     and the Division of Labor, Lloyd, Cynthia B., ed.
     (New York: Columbia University Press, 1975), pp.
     27-60

629. Fitt, Lawton Wehl and Derek A. Newton. "When the
     Mentor is a Man and the Protegee a Woman,"
     Harvard Business Review, Vol. 59 (March-April
     1981), pp. 56ff

630. Foegen, J.H. "Double Dipping the Labor Market:
     Sex-Bias Cause?" Labor Law Journal, Vol. 30
     (March 1979), pp. 181-182

631. Foner, Philip S. Women and the American Labor
     Movement: Vol 1: From Colonial Times to the Eve
     of World War I; Vol II: From World War I to the
     Present (New York: Free Press, 1979, 1980)

632. Frank, Robert H. "Why Women Earn Less: The
     Theory and Estimation of Differential
     Overqualification," American Economic Review,
     Vol. 68 (June 1978), pp. 360-373

633. Freeman, Jo, ed. "The Working Woman," in her
     Women: A Feminist Perspective (Palo Alto, CA:
     Mayfield, 1975), pp. 209-276

634. Garland, Howard and Kenneth H. Price. "Attitudes
     Toward Women in Management and Attributions for
     Their Success and Failure in a Managerial
     Position," Journal of Applied Psychology, Vol. 62
     (February 1977), pp. 29-33

635. Giele, Janet Zollinger. "Women, Men, and Work,"
     in her Women and the Future: Changing Sex Roles
     in Modern America (New York: The Free Press,
     1978), pp. 87-139, pp. 242-305

636. Giraldo, Z. I. Public Policy and the Family:
     Wives and Mothers in the Labor Force (Lexington,
     MA: D. C. Heath and Company, 1980)

637. Goldfarb, Robert S. and James R. Hosek.
     "Explaining Male-Female Wage Differentials for
     the 'Same Job,'" Journal of Human Resources, Vol.
     11 (Winter 1976), pp. 98-108

638. Goldman, Jane. "Unions, Women and Economic
     Justice: Litigating Union Sex Discrimination,"
     Women's Rights Law Reporter, Vol. 4 (Fall 1977),
     pp. 3-26

639. Gordon, H. A. and K. C. W. Kammeyer. "Gainful
     Employment of Women With Small Children," Journal
     of Marriage and the Family, Vol. 42 (May 1980),
     pp. 327-336

640. Graebner, W. "Uncle Sam Just Loves the Ladies:
     Sex Discrimination in the Federal Government,
     1917," Labor History, Vol. 21 (Winter 1979-80),
     pp. 75-85

641. Greenwald, Maurine Weiner. Women, War, and Work:
     The Impact of World War I on Women Workers in the
     United States (Westport, CT: Greenwood Press,
     1980)

642. Grossman, Allyson Sherman. "Women in Domestic
     Work: Yesterday and Today," Monthly Labor
     Review, Vol. 103 (August 1980), pp. 17-21

643. Gustafson, Kathleen; Alan Booth; and David
     Johnson. "The Effect of Labor Force
     Participation on Gender Differences in Voluntary
     Association Affiliation: A Cross-National
     Study," Journal of Voluntary Action Research,
     Vol. 8 (July-October 1979), pp. 51-56

644. Guzda, Henry P. "Francis Perkin's Interest in a
     New Deal for Blacks: The Black Oriented Programs
     of the Nation's First Female Cabinet Member May
     Seem Modest by Today's Standards; However, in Her
     Time She Was a Pioneer, Who Made the Welfare of
     Blacks a Priority of the Department of Labor,"
     Monthly Labor Review, Vol. 103 (April 1980), pp.
     31-35

645. Hacker, Sally. "Sex, Stratification, Technology
     and Organizational Change: A Longitudinal Case
     Study of AT&T," Social Problems, Vol. 26, No. 5
     (June 1979), pp. 539-568

646. Halaby, Charles N. "Job-Specific Sex Differences
     in Organizational Reward Attainment: Wage
     Discrimination vs. Rank Segregation," Social
     Forces, Vol. 58 (Spring 1979), pp. 108-127

647. "Head of Women's Group Discusses Fledgling Union
     (Interview with Karen Nussbaum, Executive
     Director of Working Women and Head of District
     925; On Attempts to Organize Women Office
     Workers, Particularly Female Bank Employees),"
     ABA (American Bankers Association) Banking
     Journal, Vol. 73 (November 1981), pp. 148ff

648. Heath, Anthony. "Women Who Get On in the
     World--Up to a Point," New Society, Vol. 55
     (February 12, 1981), pp. 275-278

649. Heckman, James J. and Robert J. Willis. "A
     Beta-logistic Model for the Analysis of
     Sequential Labor Force Participation by Married
     Women," Journal of Political Economy, Vol. 85
     (February 1977), pp. 27-58

650. Hennig, Margaret and Anne Jardim. The Managerial
     Woman (Garden City, NY: Doubleday, 1977)

651. Henry, James S. "Lazy, Young, Female, and Black:
     The New Conservative Theories of Unemployment,"
     New Society, Vol. 6 (May/June 1978), pp. 55-65

652. Hofferth, Sandra L. "Day Care in the Next
     Decade: 1980-1990," Journal of Marriage and the
     Family, Vol. 41 (August 1979), pp. 649-658

653. Hofferth, Sandra L. and Kristin A. Moore.
     "Women's Employment and Marriage," "Women and
     Their Children," The Subtle Revolution: Women at
     Work, Smith, Ralph E., ed. (Washington, DC: The
     Urban Institute, 1979), pp. 99-159

654. Hoffman, Lois W. and F. Ivan Nye. Working
     Mothers: An Evaluative Review of the
     Consequences for Wife, Husband, and Child (San
     Francisco, CA: Jossey-Bass, 1974)

655. Hogan, Betsy. "Blacks vs. Women: When Victims
     Collide; Minorities and Women Compete for
     Employment Gains; They Should Form a Cartel to
     Enlarge the Gains," Business and Society
     Review/Innovation, No. 10 (Summer 1974), pp.
     71-77

656. Holmstrom, N. "'Women's Work,' the Family and
     Capitalism," Science and Society, Vol. 45 (Summer
     1981), pp. 186-211

657. Howe, Louise Kapp. Pink Collar Workers (New
     York: Putnam, 1977)

658. Huber, Joan, ed. Changing Women in a Changing
     Society (Chicago: Chicago University Press,
     1973)

659. Hudi, P. M. "Commitment to Work and to Family:
     Marital-Status Differences in Women's Earnings,"
     Journal of Marriage and the Family, Vol. 38 (May

1976), pp. 267-278; Discussion, Vol. 43 (May
1982), pp. 285-292

660. Inglehart, Alfreda P. Married Women and Work:
     1957-1976 (Lexington, MA: Lexington Books, 1979)

661. Iglehart, Alfreda P. "Wives, Work, and Social
     Change: What About the Housewives?" Social
     Service Review, Vol. 54 (September 1980), pp.
     317-330

662. International Ladies Garment Workers Union.
     Research Department. Conditions in the Women's
     Garment Industry (New York: International Ladies
     Garment Workers Union, January 8, 1980)

663. Janjic, Marion. "Diversifying Women's
     Employment: The Only Road to Genuine Equality of
     Opportunity," International Labor Relations, Vol.
     120 (March-April 1981), pp. 149-163

664. Johnson, B. L. "Marital and Family
     Characteristics in the Labor Force," Monthly
     Labor Review, Vol. 103 (March 1979), pp. 48-52

665. Johnson, Carolyn. "Women and Retirement: A
     Study and Implications," Family Relations, Vol.
     29 (June 1980), pp. 380-385

666. Jones, Elise F. "The Impact of Women's
     Employment on Marital Fertility in the U.S.,
     1970-75," Population Studies, Vol. 35 (July
     1981), pp. 161-173

667. Kahn-Hut, Rachel. Women and Work: Problems and
     Perspectives (New York: Oxford University Press,
     1981)

668. Kahne, Hilda. "Women in the Professions: Career
     Considerations and Job Placement Techniques,"
     Journal of Economic Issues, Vol. 5 (September
     1971), pp. 28-45

669. Kamerman, Sheila. B. and Alfred. J. Kahn.
     "Day-Care Debate: A Wider View," Public
     Interest, Vol. 54 (Winter 1979), pp. 76-93

670. Kanter, Rosabeth Moss. Women and Men of the
     Corporation (New York: Basic Books, 1977)

671. Kanter, Rosabeth Moss. Work and Family in the
     United States: A Critical Review and Agenda for
     Research and Policy (New York: Russell Sage,
     1977)

672. Kennedy, Susan E. "Poverty, Respectability and
     Ability to Work," International Journal of
     Women's Studies, Vol. 2 (September-October 1979),
     pp. 401-418

673. Kennedy, Susan Estabrook. America's White
     Working-Class Women: A Historical Bibliography
     (New York: Garland Publishing, Inc., 1981)

674. Kessler-Harris, Alice. Out to Work: A History
     of Wage-Earning Women in the United States (New
     York: Oxford University Press, 1982)

675. Kessler-Harris, Alice. "Women's Wage Work as
     Myth and History," Labor History, Vol. 19 (Spring
     1978), pp. 287-307

676. Keyserling, Mary D. "The Economic Status of
     Women in the United States," American Economic
     Review, Vol. 66 (May 1976), pp. 205-212

677. Krause, Elliott A. Division of Labor: A
     Political Perspective (Westport, CT: Greenwood
     Press, 1982)

678. Kreps, Juanita. Sex in the Marketplace:
     American Women at Work (Baltimore, MD: Johns
     Hopkins University Press, 1971). Policy Studies
     in Employment and Welfare, No. 11

80   AMERICAN WOMEN AND POLITICS

679. Kuhn, Annette and Annmarie Wolpe. Feminism and
Materialism: Women and Modes of Production
(London: Routledge and Kegan Paul, 1978)

680. Kupinsky, Stanley. Working Women (New York:
Praeger, 1982)

681. "The Labor of Women: Work and Family," Signs,
Vol. 4 (Summer 1979), Special Issue

682. Landry, Bart and Margaret Platt Jendrek. "The
Employment of Wives in Middle-Class Black
Families," Journal of Marriage and the Family,
Vol. 40 (November 1978), pp. 787-797

683. Leepson, Marc. "Affirmative Action Reconsidered
(Affirmative Action to Overcome or Prevent Racial
or Sexual Discrimination in Employment and
Education; U.S.)," Editorial Research Reports,
Vol. II (July 31, 1981), pp. 555-572

684. Levitan, Sar A. and Richard S. Belous. "Working
Wives and Mothers: What Happens to Family Life,"
Monthly Labor Review, Vol. 104 (September 1981),
pp. 26-30

685. Lloyd, Cynthia B., ed. Sex, Discrimination, and
the Division of Labor (New York: Columbia
University Press, 1975)

686. Lloyd, Cynthia B. and Beth T. Niemi. The
Economics of Sex Differentials (New York:
Columbia University Press, 1979)

687. Lopata, Helena Znaniecki. Occupation: Housewife
(New York: Greenwood Press, 1980) reprint of
1971 edition

688. Loury, Glenn C. "Is Equal Opportunity Enough?"
American Economic Review, Vol. 71 (May 1981) pp.
122-126

689. Luksetich, William A. "Market Power and
     Discrimination in White-Collar Employment:
     1969-1975 (Relationship Between Measures of
     Market Power and the Employment Opportunities of
     Minorities and Women)," Review of Social Economy,
     Vol. 39 (October 1981), pp. 145-164

690. Lyle, Jerolyn R. and Jane Ross. Employment
     Patterns of Women in Corporate America
     (Lexington, MA: Lexington Books, 1973)

691. MacKinnon, Catherine A. Sexual Harassment of
     Working Women: A Case of Sex Discrimination (New
     Haven, CT: Yale University Press, 1979)

692. Mahoney, E. R. and J. G. Richardson. "Perceived
     Social Status of Husbands and Wives--The Effects
     of Labor Force Participation and Occupational
     Prestige," Sociology and Social Research, Vol. 63
     (January 1979), pp. 364-374

693. Malkiel, Burton G. and Judith A. Malkiel.
     "Male-Female Pay Differentials in Professional
     Employment," American Economic Review, Vol. 63
     (September 1973), pp. 693-705

694. Matthaei, Julie A. An Economic History of Women
     in America: Women's Work, the Sexual Division of
     Labor and the Development of Capitalism (New
     York: Schocken Books, 1982)

695. Matthaei, Julie A. "Consequences of the Rise of
     the Two-Earner Family: The Breakdown of the
     Sexual Division of Labor," American Economic
     Review, Vol. 70 (May 1980), pp. 198-202

696. Meeker, Suzanne E. "Equal Pay, Comparable Work,
     and Job Evaluation," Yale Law Journal, Vol. 90
     (January 1981), pp. 657-680

697. Milkman, Ruth. "Organizing the Sexual Division of
     Labor: Historical Perspectives on 'Women's Work'

and the American Labor Movement," Socialist
Review, Vol. 10, (January-February 1980), pp.
95-150

698. Mincer, Jacob and Solomon Polachek. "Women's
Earnings Re-Examined," The Journal of Human
Resources, Vol. 13 (Winter 1978), pp. 103-134

699. Mincer, Jacob and Solomon Polachek. "Family
Investments in Human Capital: Earnings of
Women," Journal of Political Economy, Vol. 82,
Part 2 (March 1974), pp. S76-S108 (with comment
by Otis Dudley Duncan)

700. Mindiola, T. "Cost of Being a Mexican Female
Worker in the 1970 Houston Labor Market," Aztlan,
Vol 11 (Fall 1980), pp. 231-247

701. Moroney, J.R. "Do Women Earn Less Under
Capitalism? (A Comparison of Wages in Communist
and Capitalist Countries)," Economic Journal,
Vol. 89 (September 1979), pp. 601-613

702. Morton, Peggy. "Women's Work is Never Done,"
Women Unite, Canadian Women's Education
Collective. (Toronto: Canadian Women's
Educational Press, 1972)

703. Mott, Frank L. with Steven H. Sandell; David
Schapiro; Patricia K. Brito; Timothy J. Carr;
Carol Jusenius, Peter J. Koenig; and Sylvia F.
Moore, Center for Human Resource Research, The
Ohio State University. Women, Work, and Family:
Dimensions of Change in American Society
(Lexington, MA: Lexington Books, 1978)

704. Neuse, Stephen. M. "Sex Employment Patterns in
State Government: A Case Study," State
Government, Vol. 52 (Spring 1979), pp. 52-57

705. Newland, Kathleen. Women, Men and the Division
of Labor (Washington, DC: Worldwatch Institute,
May 1980)

706. Niemi, Albert W., Jr. "Sexist Earnings
Differences: The Cost of Female Sexuality,"
American Journal of Economics and Sociology, Vol.
36 (January 1977), pp. 33-40; Reply with
rejoinder, Davis, J. C. and C. M. Hubbard. Vol.
38 (July 1979), pp. 287-292

707. Niemi, Beth T. and Cynthia B. Lloyd. "Female
Labor Supply in the Context of Inflation,"
American Economic Review, Vol. 71 (May 1981), pp.
70-75

708. Nye, Francis Ivan and Lois Wladis Hoffman, eds.
The Employed Mother in America (Westport, CT:
Greenwood Press, 1976) reprint of 1963 edition

709. Oakley, Ann. Woman's Work: The Housewife, Past
and Present (New York: Random House, 1976)

710. Oakley, Ann. The Sociology of Housework (New
York: Pantheon Books, 1975)

711. Ogden, Warren C., Jr. "Justice and the Problem
of the Volitional Victim (Commenting on efforts
to extend antidiscrimination laws passed to
protect women, blacks, and other minorities to
alchoholics, drug addicts, the obese and
homosexuals)," Labor Law Journal, Vol. 28 (July
1977), pp. 417-420

712. Olsen, David. "The (New) Cost of Being a Woman,"
Mother Jones, Vol. 2 (January 1977), pp. 13-14

713. O'Neill, June A. "Times-series Analysis of
Women's Labor Force Participation," American
Economic Review; Papers and Proceedings, Vol. 71
(May 1981), pp. 76-80

714. Oppenheimer, Valerie Kincade. The Female Labor
Force in the United States (Berkeley, CA:
Institute of International Studies, University of
California, 1970)

715. Pfeffer, Jeffrey and Jerry Ross. "Unionization
     and Female Wage and Status Attainment,"
     Industrial Relations, Vol. 20 (May 1981), pp.
     179-185

716. The Political Economy of Women, Review of Radical
     Political Economy, Vol. 12 (Summer 1980) pp. 1-94

717. Powers, Mary G. and Joan J. Holmberg.
     "Occupational Status Scores: Changes Introduced
     by the Inclusion of Women," Demography, Vol. 15
     (May 1978), pp. 183-204

718. Presser, H. B. and W. Baldwin. "Child Care as a
     Constraint on Employment: Prevalence,
     Correlates, and Bearing on the Work and Fertility
     Nexus," American Journal of Sociology, Vol. 85
     (March 1980), pp. 1202-1213

719. Quinlan, Daniel C. and Jean A. Shackelford.
     "Labor Force Participation Rates of Women and the
     Rise of the Two-Earner Family," (with reply by M.
     O. Keating), American Economic Review; Papers and
     Proceedings, Vol. 70 (May 1980), pp. 209-212

720. Rapoport, Rhona and Robert N. Rapoport. Dual
     Career Families (London: M. Robertson, 1976)

721. Ratner, Ronnie Steinberg, ed. Equal Employment
     Policy for Women: Strategies for Implementation
     in the United States, Canada and Western Europe
     (Philadelphia, PA: Temple University Press,
     1980)

722. Rein, Martin. Work for Women on Welfare (New
     York: Praeger Publishers, 1982)

723. Reuther, Rosemary. "Working Women and the Male
     Workday: Toward New Solutions," Christianity and
     Crisis, Vol. 37 (February 7, 1977), pp. 3-8

724. Robinson, Donald A. "Two Movements in Pursuit of
     Equal Employment Opportunity," Signs, Vol. 4
     (Spring 1979), pp. 413-433

725. Rosen, Benson and Thomas H. Jerdee. "Coping with Affirmative Action Backlash: Managers Must be Aware of and Find Equitable Solutions to Complaints of Favoritism from Employees Who Are Not Protected by Affirmative Action Programs—or Risk Serious Consequences," Business Horizons, Vol. 22 (August 1979), pp. 15-20

726. Rosenblum, Marc. "The Great Labor Force Projection Debate: Implications for 1980," American Economist, Vol. 16 (Fall 1973), pp. 122-129

727. Rosenfield, R. A. "Race and Sex Differences in Career Dynamics," American Sociology Review, Vol. 45 (August 1980), pp. 583-609

728. Rourke, Nancy. "The New York Telephone Settlement: A Study in Contrast," Women's Rights Law Reporter, Vol. 1 (Summer 1973), pp. 15-17

729. Rozen, Frieda Shoenberg. "Women in the Work Force: The Interaction of Myth and Reality," The Study of Women: Enlarging Perspectives of Social Reality, Snyder, Eloise B., ed. (New York: Harper & Row, 1979), pp. 79-102

730. Rupp, Leila J. Mobilizing Women for War: German and America Propaganda, 1939-1945 (Princeton, NJ: Princeton University Press, 1978)

731. Russell, Cheryl. "Women Breadwinners," American Demographics, Vol. 3 (July-August 1981), pp. 42-43

732. Safilos-Rothschild, Constantina. "A Cross Cultural Examination of Women's Marital, Educational, and Occupational Options," Acta Sociologica, Vol. 14, Nos. 1-2 (1971), pp. 96-113

733. Sandell, S. H. "Is the Unemployment Rate of Women Too Low? A Direct Test of the Economic Theory of

Job Search," Economic Statistics, Vol. 62
(November 1980), pp. 634-638

734. Sandell, Steven H. and David Shapiro. "An
Exchange: The Theory of Human Capital and the
Earnings of Women," The Journal of Human
Resources, Vol. 13 (Winter 1978), pp. 103-117

735. Sawhill, Isabel V. "The Economics of
Discrimination Against Women: Some New
Findings," Journal of Human Resources, Vol. 8
(Summer 1973), pp. 383-396

736. Scanzoni, John. Sex Roles, Women's Work, and
Marital Conflict (Lexington, MA: Lexington
Books, 1978)

737. Schreiber, Carol Tropp. Changing Places: Men
and Women in Transitional Occupations (Boston:
MIT Press, 1979)

738. Seidman, Ann, ed. Working Women: A Study of
Women in Paid Jobs (Boulder, CO: Westview Press,
1978)

739. Sekscenski, Edward S. "Women's Share of
Moonlighting Nearly Doubles During 1969-1979,"
Monthly Labor Review, Vol. 103 (May 1980), pp.
36-39

740. Semyonov, M. "Social Context of Women's Labor
Force Participation: A Comparative Analysis,"
American Journal of Sociology, Vol. 86 (November
1980), pp. 534-550

741. Shaffer, Butler D. and J. Brad Chapman. "Hiring
Quotas--Will They Work?" Labor Law Journal, Vol.
26 (March 1975), pp. 152-162

742. Shaw, Lois B. Changes in the Work Attachment of
Married Women (Columbus, OH: Center for Human
Resource Research, Ohio State University, October
1979)

Resource Research, Ohio State University, October 1979)

743. Sidel, Ruth. Urban Survival: The World of Working Class Women (New York: Beacon Press, 1978)

744. Singer, James W. "Undervalued Jobs: What's a Woman (and the Government) To Do? The Equal Employment Opportunity Commission is Considering Regulations Against a Subtle Form of Discrimination: Low Wages for Jobs held Mostly by Women," National Journal, Vol. 12, (May 24, 1980), pp. 858-862

745. Singer, James W. "It's Still Too Early to Perform Last Rites on the Sugarman Plan: The Plan to Give Women and Minorities a Leg Up On Federal Jobs Has Been Anything But Well Received; But It's Not Dead Yet," National Journal, Vol. 10 (October 21, 1978), pp. 1680-1681

746. Slotnick, Robert S. and J. Bleiberg. "Authoritarianism, Occupational Sex-Typing, and Attitudes Toward Work," Psychological Reports, Vol. 35 (October 1974), pp. 763-770

747. Smith, Ralph E., ed. The Subtle Revolution: Women at Work (Washington, DC: The Urban Institute, 1979)

748. Smuts, Robert. Women and Work in America (New York: Schocken Books, 1971)

749. Sokoloff, Natalie J. Between Money and Love: The Dialectics of Women's Home and Market Work (New York: Praeger Publishers, 1980)

750. Sorkin, Alan L. "Occupational Status and Unemployment of Nonwhite Women," Social Forces, Vol. 49 (March 1971), pp. 393-398

751. Steinberg, Ronnie. Wages and Hours: Labor and
     Reform in Twentieth Century America (New
     Brunswick, NJ: Rutgers University Press, 1982)

752. Stencel, Sandra. "Women in the Work Force,"
     Editorial Research Reports, Vol I (Feb. 18,
     1977), pp. 121-42

753. Stencel, Sandra. "Reverse Discrimination",
     Editorial Research Reports, Vol II (Aug. 6,
     1976), pp. 561-580

754. Strasser, Susan. Never Done: A History of
     American Housework (New York: Pantheon Books,
     1982)

755. Strauss, Robert P. and Francis W. Harvath. "Wage
     Rate Differences by Race and Sex in the U.S.
     Labor Market: 1960-1970," Economica, Vol. 43
     (August 1976), pp. 287-298

756. A Study of Working-Class Women in a Changing
     World (Chicago: Social Research Inc., prepared
     for MacFadden-Bartell Corp., May 1973)

757. Sweet, James A. "The Employment of Rural Farm
     Wives," Rural Sociology, Vol. 37 (December 1972),
     pp. 553-577

758. Syzmanski, Albert. "Racism and Sexism as
     Functional Substitutes in the Labor Market,"
     Sociology Quarterly, Vol. 17 (Winter 1976), pp.
     65-73

759. Taub, Nadine. "Keeping Women in Their Place:
     Stereotyping per se as a Form of Employment
     Discrimination," Boston College Law Review, Vol.
     21 (January 1980), pp. 343-418

760. Terkel, Louis (Studs). Working (New York:
     Pantheon, 1974)

761. Tuma, N. B. and P. K. Robbins. "Dynamic Model of Employment Behavior: An Application to the Seattle and Denver Income Maintenance Experiments," Econometrica, Vol. 48 (May 1980), pp. 1031-1052

762. Underwood, Lorraine A. Women in Federal Employment Programs (Washington, DC: Urban Institute, January 1979)

763. United States Bureau of the Census, Economic Surveys Division. Selected Characteristics of Women-Owned Businesses, 1977 (Washington, DC: U.S. Government Printing Office, October, 1980)

764. United States Civil Service Commission, Manpower Statistics Division. Study of Employment of Women in the Federal Government, 1975 (Washington, DC: U.S. Government Printing Office, 1976)

765. United States Congress, Joint Economic Committee, Subcommittee on Economic Growth and Stabilization. American Women Workers in a Full Employment Economy: A Compendium of Papers (Washington, DC: U.S. Government Printing Office, 1977)

766. United States Congress, Joint Economic Committee, Smith, Ralph E. Achieving the Goals of the Employment Act of 1946: Thirtieth Anniversary Review: Vol. 1, Employment: P.A. No. 6, The Impact of Macroeconomic Conditions on Employment Opportunities for Women; A Study (Washington, DC: U.S. Government Printing Office, 1977)

767. United States Congress, Senate, Committee on Labor and Human Resources. Sex Discrimination in the Workplace, 1981: Hearings on Examination of Issues Affecting Women in Our Nation's Labor Force, 97th Congress, 1st Session, January 28 and April 21, 1981 (Washington, DC: U.S. Government Printing Office, 1981)

768. United States Department of Labor, Women's
     Bureau. Women With Low Incomes (Washington, DC:
     Employment Standards Administration, Women's
     Bureau, November 1977)

769. United States Equal Employment Opportunity
     Commission. Job Patterns for Minorities and
     Women in Private Industry: Equal Employment
     Opportunity Report, 1979 (Washington, DC: U.S.
     Government Printing Office, September, 1981)

770. United States Equal Employment Opportunity
     Commission, Office of Planning, Research and
     Systems. Equal Employment Opportunity Report,
     1975: Job Patterns for Minorities and Women in
     Private Industry (Washington, DC: U.S.
     Government Printing Office, 1977)

771. Van Alstyne, Carol; Julie Withers; and Sharon
     Elliot. "Affirmative Inaction: The Bottom Line
     Tells the Tale," Change, Vol. 9 (August 1977),
     pp. 39-41, p. 60

772. Villemez, Wayne J. "The Functional
     Substitutability of Blacks and Females in the
     Labor Market: A Closer Look," The Sociological
     Quarterly, Vol. 18 (Autumn 1977), pp. 548-563

773. Waerness, K. "Invisible Welfare State: Women's
     Work at Home," Acta Sociologica, Vol. 21
     Supplement (1978), pp. 193-207

774. Waldman, Elizabeth. "Working Mothers in the
     1970's: A Look at the Statistics," Monthly Labor
     Review, Vol. 102 (October 1979), pp. 39-49

775. Wallace, Phyllis A., et al. Black Women in the
     Labor Force (Cambridge, MA: MIT Press, 1980)

776. Wallace, Phyllis A. and Annette M. La Mond, eds.
     Women, Minorities, and Employment Discrimination
     (Lexington, MA: Lexington Books, 1977)

777. Weiner, Lois. "Women Trade Unionists Organize,"
     New Politics, Vol. 11 (Winter 1974), pp. 31-35

778. Weiss, Jane A. and Francisco O. Ramirez. "Female
     Participation in the Occupational System: A
     Comparative Institutional Analysis," Social
     Problems, Vol. 23 (June 1976), pp. 593-608

779. Welch, Finis. "Affirmative Action and its
     Enforcement," American Economic Review, Vol. 71
     (May 1981), pp. 127-133

780. Wertheimer, Barbara Meyer. We Were There: The
     Story of Working Women in America (New York:
     Pantheon Books, 1977)

781. Wertheimer, Barbara Meyer and Ann H. Nelson.
     Trade Union Women: A Study of Their
     Participation in New York City Locals (New York:
     Praeger, 1975)

782. Williams, G. "Changing U.S. Labor Force and
     Occupational Differentiation by Sex," Demography,
     Vol. 16 (Fall 1979), pp. 73-87

783. Wise, Donna L. "Challenging Sexual Preference
     Discrimination in Private Employment," Ohio State
     Law Journal, Vol. 41 (November 2, 1980), pp.
     501-531

784. Wolf, Wendy C. and Neil D. Fligstein. "Sex and
     Authority in the Workplace: The Causes of Sexual
     Inequality," American Sociological Review, Vol.
     44 (April 1979), pp. 235-252

785. "Women at Work: A Special Section," Monthly
     Labor Review, Vol. 93 (June 1970), pp. 3-44

786. "Women in Trade Unions (Canada and the United
     States)," Labour Gazette (Canada), Vol. 71
     (October 1971), pp. 682-685

787. Wright, James D. "Are Working Women Really More
      Satisfied? Evidence from Several National Su-
      rveys," Journal of Marriage and the Family," Vol.
      40 (May 1978), pp. 301-313

788. Wyper, Roberta. "Back to Work as 'Temporaries,'"
      Worklife, Vol. 2 (April 1977), pp. 24-26

789. Zashin, Elliot M. "Affirmative Action and
      Federal Personnel Systems," Public Policy, Vol.
      28 (Summer 1980), pp. 351-380

VII. WOMEN AND EDUCATION

790. Abramson, Joan. The Invisible Woman:
Discrimination in the Academic Profession (San
Francisco, CA: Jossey-Bass, 1975)

791. Atkinson, Paul. "Fitness, Feminism, and
Schooling," The Nineteenth Century Woman: Her
Cultural and Physical World, Delamont, Sara and
Lorna Duffin, eds. (New York: Barnes and Noble,
1978), pp. 92-133

792. Bernard, Jessie S. Academic Women (University
Park, PA: Pennsylvania State University Press,
1974)

793. Bernard, Michael E. "Does Sex Role Behavior
Influence the Way Teachers Evaluate Students?"
Journal of Educational Psychology, Vol. 71
(August 1979), pp. 553-562

794. Bilkin, Sari Knopp and Marilyn Brannigan. Women
and Educational Leadership (Lexington, MA:
Lexington Books, 1980)

795. Blackstone, W. and R. Heslopp, eds. Social
Justice and Preferential Treatment: Women and
Racial Minorities in Education and Business
(Athens, GA: University of Georgia, 1977)

796. Carnegie Commission on Higher Education.
Opportunities for Women in Higher Education:

94 AMERICAN WOMEN AND POLITICS

Their Currrent Participation, Prospects for the
Future, and Recommendations for Action; A Report
and Recommendations (New York: McGraw-Hill,
1973)

797. Churgin, Jonah. The New Woman and the Old
Academe: Sexism and Higher Education (Roslyn
Heights, NY: Libra Publishers, 1978)

798. Cohen, Jere. "High School Subcultures and the
Adult World," Adolescence, Vol. 14 (Fall 1979),
pp.491-502

799. Conable, Charlotte Williams. Women at Cornell:
The Myth of Equal Education (Ithaca, NY: Cornell
University Press, 1977)

800. Conway, Jill K. "Perspectives on the History of
Women's Education in the United States," History
of Education Quarterly, Vol. 14 (Spring 1974),
pp. 1-12

801. Conway, Jill K. "Women Reformers and American
Culture," Journal of Social History, Vol. 5
(Winter 1971-72), pp. 164-177

802. Cook, Beverly, B. "Evaluating Textbooks for Sex
Bias," News (for Teachers of Political Science),
No. 30 (Summer 1981), pp. 1, 24

803. Delamont, Sara. "The Contradictions in Ladies'
Education," "The Domestic Ideology and Women's
Education," in her The Nineteenth Century Woman:
Her Cultural and Physical World, Delamont, Sara
and Lorna Duffin eds. (New York: Barnes and
Noble, 1978), pp. 134-187

804. Farley, Jennie, ed. Sex Discrimination in Higher
Education: Strategies of Equality (Ithaca, NY:
New York State School of Industrial Labor
Relations, Cornell University, 1981)

805. Ferber, Marianne A. and B. Kordick. "Sex
     Differentials in the Earnings of Ph.D.s.,"
     Industrial and Labor Relations, Vol. 31 (January
     1978), pp. 227-238

806. Ferber, Marianne A. and Walter W. McMahon.
     "Women's Expected Earnings and Their Investment
     in Higher Education," Journal of Human Resources,
     Vol. 14 (Summer 1979), pp. 405-420

807. Fields, Cheryl. "Women at Military Academies: A
     Report Card from Psychologists," Chronicle of
     Higher Education, Vol. 19 (August 10, 1979) pp.

808. Finn, Jeremy; Loretta Dulberg; and Janet Reis.
     "Sex Differences in Educational Attainment: A
     Cross National Perspective," Harvard Educational
     Review, Vol. 49 (November 1979), pp. 477-503

809. Fox, Lynn et al. Women and the Mathematical
     Mystique (Baltimore, MD: Johns Hopkins
     University Press, 1980)

810. Froines, Ann. "Integrating Women Into the
     Liberal Arts Curriculum: Some Results of a
     'Modest Survey,'" Women's Studies Newsletter,
     Vol. 8 (Fall-Winter 1980), pp. 11-12

811. Giele, Janet Zollinger. "Education for the
     Future," in her Women and the Future: Changing
     Sex Roles in Modern America (New York: The Free
     Press, 1978), pp. 242-305

812. Gould, Stephen Jay. The Mismeasure of Man (about
     racism and sexism in I.Q. testing) (New York:
     Norton, 1981)

813. Hoffer, Stefan N. "Private Rates of Return to
     Education for Women," Review of Economics and
     Statistics, Vol. 55 (November 1973), pp. 482-486

814. Hook, Janet. "Scholars Wage Campaign to
     Integrate Research on Women into Standard

Liberal-Arts Courses," The Chronicle of Higher
Education (November 4, 1981), p. 23

815. Hook, Janet. "Women's Studies Win Growing
Support in Fight For Academic Legitimacy,"
Chronicle of Higher Education, Vol. 21 (September
1980) pp. 3-4

816. Horner, Matina. "A Bright Woman is Caught in a
Double Bind," Psychology Today, Vol. 3 (November
1969), pp. 36-38

817. Houston, L. N. and S. I. Spainger. "Self-Esteem
and Conservatism Among Female College Students,"
Psychology Report, Vol. 47 (October 1980), pp.
543-546

818. Howe, Florence, ed. Women and the Power to
Change (New York: McGraw-Hill, 1975)

819. Jencks, Christopher et al. Inequality: A
Reassessment of the Effect of Family and
Schooling in America (New York: Harper and Row,
1973)

820. Johnson, Robert C., Jr. "Affirmative Action and
the Academic Profession," American Academy of
Political and Social Sciences Annals, Vol. 448
(March 1980), pp. 102-114

821. Kelly, Gail P. "The Schooling of Vietnamese
Immigrants: Internal Colonialism and its Impact
on Women," Comparative Perspectives of Third
World Women: the Impact of Sex, Race and Class,
Lindsay, Beverly, ed. (New York: Praeger
Publishers, 1980), pp. 276-296

822. Kersey, Shirley Nelson. Classics in the
Education of Girls and Women (Metuchen, NJ:
Scarecrow Press, 1981)

823. Ketchum, Sara. "Female Culture, Womanculture and
Conceptual Change: Toward a Philosophy of

Education   97

Women's Studies," <u>Social Theory and Practice</u>,
Vol. 6 (Summer 1980), pp. 151-162

824. Klein, Susan. <u>Sex Equity in Education</u>
(Washington, DC: The National Institute of
Education, February 1980)

825. Kutner, Nancy G. and Donna Brogan. "Sources of
Sex Discrimination in Educational System: A
Conceptual Mode," <u>Psychology of Women Quarterly</u>,
Vol. 1 (Fall 1976), pp. 50-69

826. Leepson, Marc. "Affirmative Action Reconsidered
(Affirmative Action to Overcome or Prevent Racial
or Sexual Discrimination in Employment and
Education; U.S.)," <u>Editorial Research Reports</u>,
Vol. II (July 31, 1981), pp. 555-572

827. Leinhardt, Gaea; Andrea May Seewald; and Mary
Engel. "Learning What's Taught: Sex Differences
in Instruction," <u>Journal of Educational
Psychology</u>, Vol. 11 (August 1979), pp. 432-439

828. Lougee, Carolyn C. "Women, History, and the
Humanities: An Argument in Favor of the General
Studies Curriculum," <u>Women's Studies Quarterly</u>,
Vol. 9 (Spring 1981), pp. 4-7

829. McCurdy, Jack. "University, Opposed to Lesbians,
Bars Women's Studies Meetings," <u>Chronicle of
Higher Education</u>, Vol. 22 (March 1981), p. 2

830. MacLeod, Jennifer S. and Sandra T. Silverman.
<u>"You Won't Do": What Textbooks on U.S.
Government Teach High School Girls</u> (Pittsburgh,
PA: KNOW, Inc., 1973)

831. Mednick, Martha T. S.; Sandra S. Tangri; and Lois
W. Hoffman, eds. <u>Women and Achievement: A Social
and Motivational Analysis</u> (New York: Halsted
Press, 1975), pp. 104-143

832. Mosley, Myrtis Hall. "Black Women Administrators
     in Higher Education: An Endangered Species,"
     Journal of Black Studies, Vol. 10 (March 1980),
     pp. 295-310

833. Moss, Jacque D. and Frederick G. Brown. "Sex
     Bias and Academic Performance: An Empirical
     Study," Journal of Education Management, Vol. 16
     (August 1979), pp. 197-202

834. Niemi, Albert W., Jr. "Sexist Differences in
     Returns to Educational Investment," Quarterly
     Review of Economics and Business, Vol. 15 (Spring
     1975), pp. 17-25

835. O'Connell, A. N. "Effects of Manipulated Status
     on Performance, Goal Setting Achievement
     Modification, Anxiety, and Fear of Success,"
     Journal of Social Psychology, Vol. 112 (October
     1980), pp. 75-89

836. Olsen, Nancy J. and Eleanor W. Willemsen. "Fear
     of Success--Fact or Artifact?" The Journal of
     Psychology, Vol. 98 (Janury 1978), pp. 65-70

837. Osborn, Ruth Helm. Developing New Horizons for
     Women (New York: McGraw-Hill, 1977)

838. Peplau, Lititia Anne. "Impact of Fear of Success
     and Sex-Role Attitudes on Women's Competitive
     Achievement," Journal of Personality and Social
     Psychology, Vol. 34 (October 1976), pp. 561-568

839. Perun, Pamela J., ed. The Undergraduate Woman:
     Issues in Educational Equity (Lexington, MA:
     Lexington Books, 1982)

840. Reviere, Rebecca and Thomas Posey. "Correlates
     of Two Measures of Fear of Success in Women,"
     Psychological Reports, Vol. 42 (April 1978), pp.
     609-610

841. Rich, Adrienne. "Taking Women Students
     Seriously," Radical Teacher, No. 11 (March 1979),
     pp. 40-43

842. Rich, Adrienne. "Toward a Woman-Centered
     University" in her On Lies, Secrets and Silence
     (New York: Longman, 1982), pp. 125-155

843. Roby, Pamela. "Structural and Internal Barriers
     to Women in Education," Women: A Feminist
     Perspective, Freeman, Jo, ed. (Palo Alto, CA:
     Mayfield, 1975), pp. 171-193

844. Ross, Susan C. "Education," in her The Rights of
     Women (New York: Avon, 1973), pp. 116-148

845. Rossi, Alice S., ed. Academic Women on the Move
     (New York: Russell Sage, 1973)

846. Saario, T. T. "Sexism, Inequality, and
     Education," Harvard Educational Review, Vol. 48
     (May 1978), pp. 267

847. Sadker, Myra Pollack. Sex Equity Handbook for
     Schools (New York: Longman, 1982)

848. Safilos-Rothschild, Constantina. "A Cross
     Cultural Examination of Women's Marital,
     Educational, and Occupational Options," Acta
     Sociologica, Vol. 14, Nos. 1-2 (1971), pp. 96-113

849. Sherman, Julia A. and Evelyn Torton Beck. The
     Prism of Sex: Essays in the Sociology of
     Knowledge (Madison: University of Wisconsin
     Press, 1979)

850. Smith, Carol Jo. Selected List of Postsecondary
     Opportunities for Minorities and Women
     (Washington, DC: Department of Health, Education
     and Welfare, Office of Education June 1978)

851. Stacey, Judith et al, eds. And Jill came
     Tumbling After: Sexism in American Education
     (New York: Dell Publishing Co., 1974)

852. Stebbins, Charles A.; Bryan R. Kelly; Alexander
     Tolor; and Mary Ellen Power. "Sex Differences in
     Assertiveness in College Students," The Journal
     of Psychology, Vol. 95 (March 1977), pp. 309-315

853. Steele, Diana A. "Focusing on Vocational
     Education," Civil Liberties Review, Vol. 5
     (January-February 1979), pp. 66-69

854. Stiehm, Judith Hicks. Bring Me Men and Women:
     Mandated Change at the Air Force Academy
     (Berkeley, CA: University of California Press,
     1980)

855. Synott, Marcia Graham. The Half-Opened Door:
     Discrimination and Admissions at Harvard, Yale,
     and Princeton, 1900-1970 (Westport, CT:
     Greenwood Press, 1979)

856. Tilly, Louise A. "The Social Sciences and the
     Study of Women: A Review Article," Comparative
     Studies in Society and History, Vol. 20 (January
     1978), pp. 163-173

857. Tuckman, Barbara H. and Howard P. Tuckman. "Part
     Timers, Sex Discrimination, and Career Choice at
     Two-Year Institutions: Further Findings Form the
     AAUP Survey," Academe, Vol. 66 (March 1980), pp.
     71-76

858. The Unfinished Assignment: Equal Education for
     Women (Washington, DC: Worldwatch Institute,
     July 1976)

859. United States Congress, Senate, Committee on
     Labor and Human Resources, Subcommittee on
     Health and Scientific Research. Women In Science
     and Technology Equal Opportunity Act, 1979:
     Hearings on S. 568, To Promote the Full Use of

Human Resources in Science and Technology Through
a Comprehensive Program to Maximise the Potential
Contribution and Advancement of Women In
Scientific, Professional, and Technical Careers,
96th Congress, First Session, August 1, 1979
(Washington D.C.: U.S. Government Printing
Office, 1979)

860. United States Department of Health, Education and
Welfare. Office for Civil Rights. Racial,
Ethnic and Sex Enrollment Data from Institutions
of Higher Education, Fall 1976 (Washington, DC:
U.S. Government Printing Office, April 1978)

861. United States Office of Education. Taking Sexism
Out of Education: The National Project on Women
in Education (Washington, DC: U.S. Government
Printing Office, 1978)

862. "Women and Education," Politics and Education,
Vol. 1 (Summer 1978), special edition

863. "Women and Education I," Harvard Educational
Review, Vol. 49 (November 1979), pp. 413-566

864. "Women and Education II," Harvard Educational
Review, Vol. 50 (February 1980), pp. 1-69

865. Women on Campus: The Unfinished Revolution (by
the editors of Change) (New Rochelle, NY:
Change, May 1975)

866. "Women's Influence on Education," History of
Education Quarterly, Vol. 19 (Spring 1979),
Special Issue

VIII. DEMOCRATIC POLITICAL PARTICIPATION: VOTING,
CAMPAIGN WORK, ELECTIONS

867. Amundsen, Kirsten. The Silenced Majority: Women
and American Democracy (Englewood Cliffs, NJ:
Prentice-Hall, 1971)

868. Amundsen, Kirsten. A New Look at the Silenced
Majority (Englewood Cliffs, NJ: Prentice-Hall,
1977)

869. Andersen, Kristi. "Working Women and Political
Participation 1952-1972," American Journal of
Political Science, Vol. 19 (August 1975), pp.
439-453

870. Baxter, Sandra and Marjorie Lansing. Women and
Politics: The Invisible Majority (Ann Arbor, MI:
University of Michigan Press, 1980)

871. Bayes, Jane H. Minority Politics and Ideologies
in the United States (Novato, CA: Chandler and
Sharp, 1982)

872. Bernard, Jessie. Women and the Public Interest:
An Essay on Policy and Protest (Chicago:
Aldine-Atherton Press, 1971)

873. Bokemeier, J. L. and J. L. Tait. "Women as Power
Actors: A Comparative Study of Rural
Communities," Rural Sociology, Vol. 45 (Summer
1980), pp. 238-255

874. Bourque, Susan C. and Jean Grossholtz. "Politics
     as an Unnatural Practice: Political Science
     Looks at Female Participation," Politics and
     Society, Vol. 4 (Winter 1974), pp. 225-266

875. Bryce, H. and A. Warrick. "Black Women in
     Electoral Politics," A Portrait of Marginality:
     The Political Behavior of the American Women,
     Githens, Marianne and Jewel R. Prestage, eds.
     (New York: David McKay Co., 1977), pp. 395-401

876. Burns, Ruth Ann. "Women in Municipal
     Management," Urban Data Service Reports, Vol. 12
     (February 1980), pp. 1-12

877. Costello, Mary. "Women Voters," Editorial
     Research Reports, Vol. II (October 11, 1972), pp.
     765-784

878. Cummings, Bernice and Victoria Schuck. Women
     Organizing: An Anthology (Metuchen, NJ:
     Scarecrow Press, 1979)

879. Eckert, W. A. "Impact of Candidate's Sex on
     Voter Choice," Western Political Quarterly, Vol.
     34 (March 1981), pp. 78-87

880. Evans, Judith. "Women and Politics: A
     Re-Appraisal," Political Studies, Vol. 28 (June
     1980), pp. 210-221

881. Falco, Maria J. "Bigotry!": Ethnic Machine, and
     Sexual Politics in a Senatorial Election
     (Westport, CT: Greenwood Press, 1980)

882. Feltner, Paula and Leneen Goldie. "Impact of
     Socialization and Personality on the Female
     Voter," Western Political Quarterly, Vol. 27
     (December 1974), pp. 680-692

883. Fowlkes, Diane et al. "Gender Roles and Party
     Roles," The American Political Science Review,
     Vol. 73 (September 1979), pp. 772-780

884. Fulenwider, Claire Knoche. "Feminist Ideology and the Political Attitudes and Participation of White and Minority Women," Western Political Quarterly, Vol. 34 (March 1981), pp. 17-30

885. Gelb, Joyce and Marian Lief Palley. "Women and Interest Group Politics: A Comparative Analysis of Federal Decision-Making," The Journal of Politics, Vol. 41 (May 1979), pp. 362-392

886. Gelb, Joyce and Marian Lief Palley. "Women and Interest Group Politics: A Case Study of the Equal Credit Opportunity Act," American Politics Quarterly, Vol. 5 (July 1977), pp. 331-352

887. Githens, Marianne and Jewel L. Prestage. A Portrait of Marginality: The Political Behavior of the American Woman (New York: David McKay Co., Inc., 1977)

888. Hansen, Susan B. et al. "Women's Political Participation and Policy Preferences," Social Science Quarterly, Vol. 56 (March 1976), pp. 576-590

889. Hershey, Marjorie R. and John L. Sullivan. "Sex-Role Attitudes, Identities, and Political Ideology," Sex Roles, Vol. 3 (February 1977), pp. 37-57

890. Hershey, Marjorie R. "The Politics of Androgyny? Sex Roles and Attitudes Toward Women in Politics," American Politics Quarterly, Vol. 5 (July 1977), pp. 261-287

891. Jennings, M. Kent and Barbara G. Farah. "Ideology, Gender, and Political Action: A Cross-National Survey," British Journal of Political Science, Vol. 10 (July 1980), pp. 219-240

892. Karnig, Albert K. and Susan Welch. "Sex and Ethnic Differences in Municipal Representation,"

Social Science Quarterly, Vol. 60 (December 1979), pp. 465-481

893. Keith, Pat M. "Sex Differences in Correlation of Political Activity Among the Aged," Journal of Voluntary Action Research, Vol. 7 (Summer-Fall 1978), pp. 55-64

894. Klobus-Edwards, Patricia A. and John N. Edwards. "Women as Citizen Participants: The Case of Blacks and Whites," Journal of Voluntary Action Research, Vol. 8 (July-October 1979), pp. 43-50

895. Krauss, Wilma Rule. "Political Implications of Gender Roles: A Review of the Literature," American Political Science Review, Vol. 68 (December 1974), pp. 1706-1723

896. Lansing, Marjorie. "The American Woman: Voter and Activist," Women in Politics, Jaquette, Jane S., ed (New York: Wiley, 1974), pp. 5-24

897. Levitt, Morris. "The Political Role of American Women," Journal of Human Relations, Vol. 15 (1967), pp. 23-35

898. Lynn, Naomi B. "Women in American Politics: An Overview," Women: A Feminist Perspective, Freeman, Jo, ed. (Palo Alto, CA: Mayfield, 1975), pp. 364-385

899. Lynn, Naomi B. and Cornelia Flora. "Motherhood and Political Participation: The Changing Sense of Self," Journal of Political and Military Sociology, Vol. 1 (Spring 1973), pp. 91-103

900. Margolis, Diane Rothbard. "The Invisible Hands: Sex Roles and the Division of Labor in Two Local Political Parties," Social Problems, Vol. 26 (February 1979), pp. 314-324

901. McCourt, Kathleen. Working Class Women and Grassroots Politics (Bloomington, IN: Indiana University Press, 1977)

902. Nagel, Stuart and Lenore Weitzman. "Sex and the Unbiased Jury," Judicature, Vol. 56 (October 1972), pp. 108-111

903. Newland, Kathleen. Women in Politics: A Global Review (Washington, DC: Worldwatch Institute, 1975)

904. O'Connor, Karen. Women's Organizations' Use of the Courts (Lexington, MA: Lexington Books, 1980)

905. Paizis, Suzanne. Getting Her Elected: A Political Woman's Handbook (Sacramento, CA: Creative Editions, 1977)

906. Porter, Kirk Herald. A History of Suffrage in the United States (Chicago: Greenwood Press, 1969), reprint of 1918 edition

907. Reid, Inez Smith. "Together" Black Women, Prepared for the Black Women's Community Development Foundation (New York: Third Press, 1975)

908. Salper, Roberta, ed. Female Liberation, History, and Current Politics, (New York: Knopf, 1972)

909. Sapiro, Virginia. "When are Interests Interesting? The Problem of Political Representation of Women," American Political Science Review, Vol. 75 (September 1981), pp. 701-716 with comment by Irene Diamond and Nancy Hartsock, pp. 717-721

910. Scaturo, Douglas J. "Issue Relevance as a Source of Political Involvement," The Journal of Social Psychology, Vol. 101 (February 1977), pp. 59-67

911. Soule, John W. and Wilma E. McGrath. "A
     Comparative Study of Male-Female Political
     Attitudes at Citizen and Elite Levels," A
     Portrait of Marginality, Githens, M. and J. L.
     Prestage, eds. (New York: McKay, 1977) pp.
     178-196

912. Staudt, K. A. "Class and Sex in the Politics of
     Women Farmers," Journal of Politics, Vol. 41 (May
     1979), pp. 492-512

913. Stewart, Debra W., ed. Women in Local Politics
     (Metuchen, NJ: Scarecrow Press, 1980)

914. Stewart, Debra W. The Women's Movement in
     Community Politics in the U.S.: The Role of
     Local Commissions in the Status of Women (New
     York: Pergamon Press, 1980)

915. "Symposium on Women and Politics," Journal of
     Politics, Vol. 41 (May 1979), pp. 361-524, Whole
     Issue

916. Tedin, Kent L. et al. "Sex Differences in
     Political Attitudes and Behavior: Situational
     Factors," Journal of Politics, Vol. 38 (May 1977)
     pp. 448-456

917. Tolchin, Susan and Martin Tolchin. Clout,
     Womanpower and Politics (New York: Coward,
     McMann and Geoghegan, 1974)

918. "The Uncertain Future of Women's Commissions:
     Commissions on the Status of Women Have Well
     Proved Their Usefulness Since John Kennedy
     Established the First One in 1961; But now both
     State and Local Commission are Threatened on
     Several Fronts," Graduate Woman, Vol. 74
     (May-June 1980), pp. 10-15

919. Walters, Robert. "Political Focus: The Year of
     the Woman?" (Significant gains anticipated by
     women in 1974 elections particularly in

governorships and seats in the House and the
Senate), National Journal Reports, Vol. 6
(November 2, 1974), p. 1660

920. Welch, S. and P. Secret. "Sex, Race and
Political Participation," Western Political
Quarterly, Vol. 34 (March 1981), pp. 5-16

921. Welch, Susan. "Women as Political Animals? A
Test of Some Explanations for Male-Female
Political Participation Differences," American
Journal of Political Science, Vol. 21 (November
1977), pp. 771-730

922. West, Guida. The National Welfare Rights
Organization: The Social Protest of Poor Women
(New York: Praeger Publishers, 1981)

923. Young, Louise M. "Women's Place in American
Politics: The Historical Perspective," Journal
of Politics, Vol. 38 (August 1976), pp. 295-335

IX. DEPENDENT POLITICAL PARTICIPATION: WOMEN AS
    CLIENTS OF THE STATE

924. Almquist, Elizabeth M. "Untangling the Effects
     of Race and Sex: The Disadvantaged Status of
     Black Women," Social Science Quarterly, Vol. 56
     (June 1975), pp. 129-142

925. AuClaire, Philip A. "The Mix of Work and Welfare
     Among Long-Term AFDC Recipients," Social Service
     Review, Vol. 53 (December 1974), pp. 586-605

926. Ball, Robert M. "Are Women and Minority Groups
     Treated Fairly?" In his Social Security Today and
     Tomorrow (New York: Columbia University Press,
     1978), pp. 311-328

927. Burkhauser, Richard V. "Are Women Treated Fairly
     in Today's Social Security System?" The
     Gerontologist, Vol. 19 (June 1979), pp. 147-176

928. Chafe, William H. "Sex and Race: The Analogy of
     Social Control," The Massachusetts Review, Vol.
     18 (Spring 1977), pp. 147-176

929. Chrissinger, M. S. "Factors Affecting Employment
     of Welfare Mothers," Social Work, Vol. 25
     (January 1980), pp. 52-56

930. Christie, Claudia M. "Who's Watching the
     Children? The Cost and Availability of Day Care
     Facilities are Crucial Issues to Women Who

Work—And to Companies That Want to Welcome Women to Their Workforce," New England Business, Vol. 3 (October 5, 1981), pp. 21-23

931. Day, Phyllis J. "Sex-Role Stereotypes and Public Assistance," Social Science Review, Vol. 53 (March 1979), pp. 106-115

932. Epstein, Cynthia Fuchs. "Black and Female: The Double Whammy," Psychology Today, Vol. 7 (August 1973), pp. 57-61

933. Gelb, Joyce and Marian Lief Palley. "Women and Interest Group Politics: A Case Study of the Equal Credit Opportunity Act," American Politics Quarterly, Vol. 5 (July 1977), pp. 331-352

934. Goodsell, Charles T., ed. The Public Encounter: Where Citizen and State Meet (Bloomington, IN: Indiana University Press, 1981)

935. Gordon, Nancy M. "Institutional Responses: The Social Security System," The Subtle Revolution: Women at Work, Smith, Ralph E. ed. (Washington, DC: The Urban Institute, 1979), pp. 223-257

936. Grad, Susan. "Impact on Widows of Proposed Changes in OASI (Old-Age and Survivors Insurance) Mother's Benefits (Impact of a proposal that would terminate mother's and father's benefits when the young child in care of the surviving spouse reaches age 16, rather than age 18, as in current law)," Social Security Bulletin, Vol. 44 (February 1981), pp. 3-18

937. Hendricks, Michael and Richard Bootzin. "Race and Sex as Stimuli for Negative Affect and Physical Avoidance," Journal of Social Psychology, Vol. 98 (February 1976), pp. 111-120

938. Henley, Nancy M. and Fred Pincus. "Interrelationship of Sexist, Racist, and Anti-homosexual

Attitudes," Psychological Reports, Vol. 42
(February 1978), pp. 83-90

939. Hosek, James R. "Determinants of Family
Participation in the AFDC-Unemployed Fathers
Program," Review of Economics and Statistics,
Vol. 62 (August 1980), pp. 466-469

940. Husby, Ralph D. "Day Care for Families on Public
Assistance: Workfare Versus Welfare," Industrial
and Labor Relations Review, Vol. 27 (July 1974),
pp. 500-510

941. Iglitzin, Lynne B. "A Case Study in Patriarchal
Politics: Women on Welfare," A Portrait of
Marginality: The Political Behavior of the
American Woman, Githens, Marianne and Jewel L.
Prestage, eds. (New York: David McKay, Inc.
1977), pp. 96-112

942. Jackson, Larry R. "Welfare Mothers and Black
Liberation," Black Scholar, Vol. 1 (April 1970),
pp. 31-38

943. Joffe, Carole E. Friendly Intruders: Childcare
Professionals and Family Life (Berkeley, CA:
University of California Press, 1977)

944. Katz, Daniel et al. Bureaucratic Encounters (Ann
Arbor, MI: Institute for Social Research,
University of Michigan, 1975)

945. Kessler, R. C. et al. "Sex Differences in
Psychiatric Help-Seeking Evidence from Four
Large-Scale Surveys," Journal of Health and
Social Behaviour, Vol. 22 (March 1981), pp. 49-64

946. Kulka, R.A. et al. "Social Class and the Use of
Professional Help for Personal Problems: 1957
and 1976," Journal of Health and Social Behavior,
Vol. 20 (March 1979), pp. 2-17

947. Leo, Andre. "AFDC: Marriage to the State,"
     Radical Feminism, Koedt, Anne; Ellen Levine; and
     Anita Rapone, eds. (New York: Quadrangle Books,
     1973), pp. 222-227

948. Levine, Adeline. Love Canal: The Social
     Toxicity of Chemical Wastes (Lexington, MA:
     Lexington Books, 1981)

949. Lipsky, Michael. Street-Level Bureaucracy:
     Dilemmas of the Individual in Public Services
     (New York: Russell Sage Foundation, 1980)

950. Marsh, J.C. "Help Seeking Among (Heroin) Addicted
     and Non-addicted Women of Low Socioeconomic
     Status," Social Service Review, Vol. 54 (June
     1980), pp. 239-248

951. Masi, Dale A. Organizing for Women: Issues,
     Strategies, and Services (Lexington, MA:
     Lexington Books, 1981)

952. Mechanic, David. "Sex, Illness, Behavior, and the
     Use of Health Services," Journal of Human Stress,
     Vol. 2 (December 1976), pp. 29-40

953. Milwaukee County Welfare Rights Organization.
     Welfare Mothers Speak Out: We Ain't Gonna
     Shuffle Anymore (New York: Norton, 1972)

954. Morgan, B. "Four Pennies to My Name: What It's
     Like on Welfare," Public Welfare, Vol. 37 (Spring
     1979), pp. 13-22

955. Mudrick, N.R. "The Use of AFDC By Previously
     High- and Low-income Households," Social Service
     Review, Vol. 52 (March 1978), pp. 107-115

956. Nelson, Barbara J. "Client Evaluations of Social
     Programs," The Public Encounter, Goodsell,
     Charles T., ed. (Bloomington, IN: Indiana
     University Press, 1981), pp. 23-42

957. Nelson, Barbara J. "Helpseeking From Public
     Authorities: Who Arrives at the Agency Door?"
     Policy Sciences, Vol. 12 (August 1980), pp.
     175-192

958. Nichols, Abigail C. "Why Welfare Mothers Work:
     Implications for Employment and Training
     Services," Social Service Review, Vol. 53 (Spring
     1979), pp. 378-391

959. Piven, Frances Fox and Richard A. Cloward. Poor
     Peoples' Movements: Why They Succeed, How They
     Fail (New York: Random House, 1979)

960. Piven, Frances Fox and Richard A. Cloward.
     Regulating the Poor (New York: Vintage Books,
     1971)

961. Placek, Paul J. and Gerry E. Hendershot. "Public
     Welfare and Family Planning: An Empirical Study
     of the 'Brood Sow' Myth," Social Problems, Vol.
     21 (June 1974), pp. 658-673

962. Rein, Martin. "The Strange Care of Public
     Dependency," Transaction, Vol. 2 (March-April
     1965), pp. 16-23

963. Rogers, Gayle Thompson. "Aged Widows and OASDI
     (Old-age, Survivors, and Disability Insurance):
     Age At, and Economic Status Before and After,
     Receipt of Benefits," Social Security Bulletin,
     Vol. 44 (March 1981), pp. 3-19

964. Ross, Heather L. and Isabel V. Sawhill. "Welfare
     and Female-Headed Families" in their Time of
     Transition: The Growth of Families Headed by
     Women (Washington, DC: The Urban Institute,
     1975), pp. 93-129

965. Rothman, Barbara Katz. Women and Power in the
     Birthplace (New York: W. W. Norton and Co.,
     1982)

966. Rubin, C. L. "Response of Low Income Women and
     Abortion Facilities to Restriction of Public
     Funds for Abortion: A Study of a Large
     Metropolitan Area," American Journal of Public
     Health, Vol. 69 (Spring 1979), pp. 948-949

967. Sass, Tim. "Demographic and Economic
     Characteristics of Nonbeneficiary Widows: An
     Overview," Social Security Bulletin, Vol. 42
     (November 1979), pp. 3-14

968. Schloper, J. H. and M. J. Galinsky. "Role
     Playing: Insights and Answers for Welfare
     Clients," Public Welfare, Vol. 37 (Spring 1979),
     pp. 233-32

969. Schmidt, Stuart M. "Client-Oriented Evaluation of
     Public Agency Effectiveness," Administration and
     Society, Vol. 8 (February 1977), pp. 403-22

970. Smedley, Larry. "Maintaining the Balance in
     Social Security (Financing Problems, Relation to
     Private Pension Plans, Retirement Provision and
     Women in the System)," American Federationist,
     Vol. 86 (February 1979), pp. 20-25

971. Smith, Audrey D. and William J. Reid. "Child
     Care Arrangements of AFDC Mothers in the Work
     Incentive Program," Child Welfare, Vol. 52
     (December 1973), pp. 651-661

972. Stone, Clarence N. "Paternalism Among Social
     Agency Employees," Journal of Politics, Vol. 39
     (August 1977), pp. 794-804

973. Tillmon, Johnnie. "Welfare is a Woman's Issue,"
     Ms., (Spring 1972), pp. 111-117, Preview Issue

974. United States Congress, House of Representatives,
     Select Committee on Aging, Subcommittee on
     Retirement Income and Employment. Treatment of
     Women Under Social Security; Hearings Before the
     Task Force on Social Security and Women, 96th

Dependent Political Participation   117

Congress, 1st Session, May 16-September 13, 1979
(Washington, DC: U.S. Government Printing
Office, 1980)

975. United States Social Security Administration,
Office of Policy, Office of Research and
Statistics. "--Thy Father and Thy Mother--": A
Second Look at Filial Responsibility and Family
Policy; A reevaluation of Current Practice of
Filial Responsibility in the United States Two
Decades Later and its Relationship to the
Changing Social Security Programs, (Washington,
DC: U.S. Government Printing Office, July 1980)

976. Veroff, J. R. "Dynamics of Help-Seeking in Men
and Women: A National Survey Study," Psychiatry,
Vol. 44 (August 1981), pp. 189-200

977. West, Guida. The National Welfare Rights
Movement: The Social Protest of Poor Women (New
York: Praeger Publishers, 1981)

978. Wispe, L. and J. Kiecolt. "Victim Attractiveness
as a Function of Helping and Nonhelping," Journal
of Social Psychology, Vol. 112 (October 1980),
pp. 67-73

X. WOMEN AND POLITICAL LEADERSHIP

979. Bartol, Kathryn N. "The Effect of Male Versus Female Leaders on Follower Satisfaction and Performance," Journal of Business Research, Vol. 3 (January 1975), pp. 33-42

980. Bers, Trudy Haffron and Susan Gluck Mezey. "Support for Feminist Goals Among Leaders of Women's Community Groups," Signs, Vol. 6 (Summer 1981), pp. 737-748

981. Bokemeier, J. L. and J. L. Tait. "Women as Power Actors: A Comparative Study of Rural Communities," Rural Sociology, Vol. 45 (Summer 1980), pp. 238-255

982. Bullock, Charles S. and Patricia Lee Findley Heys. "Recruitment of Women in Congress: A Research Note," A Portrait of Marginality: The Political Behavior of the American Woman, Githens, Marianne, and Jewel L. Prestage, eds. (New York: David McKay Co., 1977), pp. 210-220

983. Calkin, Homer L. Women in American Foreign Affairs (Washington, DC: U.S. Government Printing Office, August 1977)

984. Caraway, Hattie Wyatt. Silent Hattie Speaks: The Personal Journal of Senator Hattie Caraway, Kincaid, Diane D., ed. (Westport, CT.: Greenwood Press, 1979)

985. Cayer, N. J. and L. Sigelman. "Minorities and
     Women in State and Local Government: 1973-1975,"
     Public Administration Review, Vol. 40 (Spring
     1980), pp. 443-450

986. Chafetz, Janet Saltzman and Barbara Bovee Polk.
     "Room at the Top: Social Recognition of British
     and American Females Over Time (Recognition of
     women in 'Who's Who' and 'Who's Who in America'
     in 1925 and 1965)," Social Science Quarterly,
     Vol. 54 (March 1974), pp. 843-853

987. Chamberlain, Hope. A Minority of Members: Women
     in the U.S. Congress (New York: Mentor, 1973)

988. "City Councilwomen: A Different Perspective;
     Women Find Equality in Elective Office But Also a
     Male Reluctance to Accept Their Viewpoints,"
     Nation's Cities, Vol. 11 (September 1973), pp.
     24-28

989. Clark, Albert P. "Women at the Service Academies
     and Combat Leadership," Strategic Review, Vol. 5
     (Fall 1977), pp. 64-73

990. Clarke, Harold D. and Allan Kornberg. "Moving Up
     the Political Escalator: Women Party Officials
     in the United States and Canada," The Journal of
     Politics, Vol. 41 (1979), pp. 442-477

991. Cohodas, Nadine. "First Woman To Serve: Senate
     Confirms O'Conner as Supreme Court Justice,"
     (September 21, 1981)," Congressional Quarterly
     Weekly Report, Vol. 39 (September 26, 1981), p.
     1831

992. Cole, Jonathan R. Fair Science: Women in the
     Scientific Community (New York: The Free Press,
     1979)

993. Colon, Frank T. "The Elected Woman," Social
     Studies, Vol. 58 (November 1967), pp. 256-261

994. Constantini, Edmond and Kenneth H. Craik.
     "Women as Politicians: The Social Background,
     Personality, and Political Careers of Female
     Party Leaders," A Portrait of Marginality: The
     Political Behavior of the American Woman,
     Githens, Marianne, and Jewel R. Prestage, eds.
     (New York: David McKay, Inc., 1977), pp.
     221-240

995. Cummings, Judith. "Black Women in Public Life:
     Distinctly Personal Responses Mark the Pioneers'
     Reactions to the Pressure and Demands of High
     Government Positions," Black Enterprise, Vol. 5
     (August 1974), pp. 33-35

996. Darcy, R. and Sarah Slavin. "When Women Run
     Against Men," Public Opinion Quarterly, Vol. 41
     (Spring 1977), pp. 1-12

997. Demokovich, Linda E. "From Public Interest
     Advocates to Administration Defenders: Some of
     the Men and Women Who Left the Public Interest
     Movement to Join the Administration Say Life
     Inside is Frustrating But Rewarding," National
     Journal, Vol. 10 (November 25, 1978), pp.
     1892-1898

998. Diamond, Irene. Sex Roles in the State House
     (New Haven, CT: Yale University Press, 1977)

999. Dubeck, Paula J. "Women and Access to Political
     Office: Comparison of Female and Male State
     Legislators," The Sociological Quarterly, Vol.
     17 (Winter 1976), pp. 42-52

1000. Dybkjaer, Lone. "Now You're Being Unwomanly,"
     Scandinavian Review, Vol. 65 (September 1977),
     pp. 66-70

1001. Epstein, Cynthia Fuchs. Woman's Place: Options
     and Limitations in Professional Careers
     (Berkeley, CA: University of California Press,
     1970)

1002. Epstein, Cynthia Fuchs and Rose Laub Coser, eds.
      Access to Power: Cross-National Studies of
      Women and Elites (London: Allen and Unwin,
      1980)

1003. Epstein, Laurily K., ed. Women in the
      Professions (Lexington, MA: Lexington Books,
      1975)

1004. Fadely, Nancie, Ruth B. Mandel and Rita Triviz:
      "Running for Office—Handbook from the Front
      Lines," Ms., Vol. 9 (May 1981), pp. 75-78

1005. Ferree, Myra M. "A Woman For President?
      Changing Responses, 1958-1972," Public Opinion
      Quarterly, Vol. 38 (Fall 1974), pp. 390-399

1006. Frankovic, Kathleen A. "Sex and Voting in the
      U.S. House of Representatives, 1961-1975,"
      American Politics Quarterly, Vol. 5 (July 1977),
      pp. 315-330

1007. Gelb, Joyce and Marian Lief Palley. "Women and
      Interest Group Politics: A Comparative Analysis
      of Federal Decision-Making," The Journal of
      Politics, Vol. 41 (February 1979), pp. 362-392

1008. Gelb, Joyce and Marian Lief Palley. "Women and
      Interest Group Politics: A Case Study of the
      Equal Credit Opportunity Act," American Politics
      Quarterly, Vol. 5 (July 1977), pp. 331-352

1009. Gertzog, Irwin N. and Michel M. Simard. "Women
      and 'Hopeless' Congressional Candidacies:
      Nomination Frequency, 1916-1978," American
      Politics Quarterly, Vol. 9 (October 1981), pp.
      449-466

1010. Gertzog, Irwin N. "The Martrimonial Connection:
      The Nomination of Congressmen's Widows for the
      House of Representatives," Journal of Politics,
      Vol. 42 (August 1980), pp. 820-833

Political Leadership   123

1011. Githens, Marianne and Jewel Prestage. "Women
      State Legislators: Styles and Priorities,"
      Policy Studies Journal, Vol. 7 (Winter 1978),
      pp. 264-270

1012. Gruberg, Martin. Women in American Politics:
      An Assessment and Source Book (Oshkosh, WI:
      Academia Press, 1968)

1013. Gruhl, J. et al. "Women as Policymakers: The
      Case of Trial Judges," American Journal of
      Political Science, Vol. 25 (May 1981), pp.
      308-22

1014. Haberman, Nancy and Ann Northrop. "The Fresh-
      women in Congress," Ms., Vol. 7 (January 1979),
      p. 58

1015. Hangen, Barbara, ed. for the United States
      Interdepartmental Taskforce on Women. Women: A
      Documentary of Progress During the
      Administration of Jimmy Carter, 1977 to 1981.
      (Washington, DC: Executive Office of the
      President, 1981)

1016. Harris, Barbara J. Beyond Her Sphere: Women
      and the Professions in American History
      (Westport, CT: Greenwood Press, 1978)

1017. Hedlund, Ronald D. et al. "The Electibility of
      Women Candidates: The Effects of Sex-Role
      Stereotypes," The Journal of Politics, Vol. 41
      (1979), pp. 513-524

1018. Heller, Trudy. Women and Men as Leaders:
      Contemporary Images (New York: Praeger, 1981)

1019. Hennig, Margaret and Ann Jardim. The Managerial
      Woman (New York: Anchor Press, 1977)

1020. Hill, D. B. "Political Culture and Female
      Political Representation," Journal of Politics,
      Vol. 43 (February 1981), pp. 159-168

1021. Holsti, Ole R. and James N. Rosenau. "The
      Foreign Policy Beliefs of Women in Leadership
      Positions," Journal of Politics, Vol. 43 (May
      1981), pp. 326-47

1022. Howard, L. C. "Civil Service Reform: A
      Minority and Woman's Perspective," Public
      Administrative Review, Vol. 38 (July 1978), pp.
      305-309. Reply with rejoinder: Campbell, A.
      K., Vol. 38 (November 1978), pp. 605-606

1023. Huerta, Faye C. and Thomas A. Lane.
      "Participation of Women in Centers of Power,"
      Social Science Journal, Vol. 18 (April 1981),
      pp. 71-86

1024. "In Their Own Words: Top Women Bureaucrats Talk
      About Jobs, Bias, and Their Changing Roles,"
      U.S. News, Vol. 83 (September 1977), pp. 38-40

1025. Jennings, M. Kent and Norman Thomas. "Men and
      Women in Party Elites: Social Roles and
      Political Resources," Midwest Journal of
      Political Science, Vol. 12 (November 1968), pp.
      469-492

1026. Joffe, Carole E. Friendly Intruders: Childcare
      Professionals and Family Life (Berkeley, CA:
      University of California Press, 1977)

1027. Johnson, Marilyn; and Kathy Stanwick.
      "Statistical Essay: Profile of Women Holding
      Office," Women and Public Office: A Bio-
      graphical Directory and Statistical Analysis,
      compiled by Center for the American Woman and
      Politics, Rutgers University, New Brunswick, New
      Jersey (Metuchen, NJ: Scarecrow Press, 1978)

1028. Kanter, Rosabeth Moss. Women and Men of The
      Corporation (New York: Basic Books, 1977)

1029. Karnig, Albert K. and B. O. Walter. "Election
      of Women to City Councils," Social Science
      Quarterly, Vol. 56 (March 1976), pp. 605-613

1030. Karnig, Albert K. and Susan Welch. "Sex and
      Ethnic Differences in Municipal Representation,"
      Social Science Quarterly, Vol. 60 (December
      1979), pp. 465-481

1031. Kelly, Rita Mae and Mary Boutillier. The Making
      of Political Women: A Study of Socialization
      and Role Conflict (Chicago: Nelson-Hall, 1977)

1032. Kincaid, D. D. "Over His Dead Body: A Positive
      Perspective on Widows in the U. S. Congress,"
      Western Political Quarterly, Vol. 31 (March
      1978), pp. 96-104

1033. Kirkpatrick, Jeane S. The New Presidential
      Elite: Men and Women in National Politics (New
      York: Basic Books, 1976)

1034. Kirkpatrick, Jeane S. Political Woman (New York:
      Basic Books, 1974)

1035. Kirschten, Dick. "Reagan's Approch to Women's
      Issues—Let Them Simmer on the Back Burner: The
      President has Appointed Few Women to Top Posts
      in His Administration, and He Has Been Slow to
      Support Legislation Proposals to Eliminate Sex
      Discrimination," National Journal, Vol. 13 (May
      1981), pp. 926-927

1036. Kohn, Walter S. G. Women in National
      Legislatures: A Comparative Study of Six
      Countries (New York: Praeger 1980)

1037. Lamson, Peggy. Few Are Chosen: American Woman
      in Political Life Today (Boston: Houghton
      Mifflin, 1968)

1038. Larwood, Laurie and Marian M. Wood. Women in
      Management (Lexington, MA: Lexington Books,
      1977)

1039. Lee, Marcia M. "Toward Understanding Why Few
      Women Hold Public Office: Factors Affecting the
      Participation of Women in Local Politics," A
      Portrait of Marginality: The Political Behavior
      of the American Woman, Githens, Marianne and
      Jewel R. Prestage, eds. (New York: David McKay,
      Inc., 1977), pp. 118-138

1040. Lepper, Mary M. "A Study of Career Patterns of
      Federal Executives: A Focus on Women," Women in
      Politics, Jaquette, Jane S., ed. (New York:
      Wiley, 1974), pp. 109-130

1041. McCourt, Kathleen. Working-Class Women and
      Grass-Roots Politics (Bloomington, IN: Indiana
      University Press, 1977)

1042. McGrath, Wilma E. and John W. Soule. "Rocking
      the Cradle or Rocking the Boat: Women at the
      1972 Democratic National Convention," Social
      Science Quarterly, Vol. 55 (June 1974), pp.
      141-150

1043. MacManus, S. A. "City's First Female
      Officeholder: Coattails for Future Female
      Officeseekers?," Western Political Quarterly,
      Vol. 34 (March 1981), pp. 88-99

1044. Mandel, Ruth B. In the Running: The New Woman
      Candidate (New Haven, CT: Ticknor and Fields,
      1981)

1045. Markoff, Helen S. "The Federal Women's Program
      (Established in 1967 to enhance employment and
      advancement opportunities for women in the
      federal government, and integrated by a 1969
      executive order into the Equal Employment
      Opportunities Program)," Public Administration
      Review, Vol. 32 (March-April 1972), pp. 144-151

1046. Mattfeld, Jacquelyn A. and Carol G. Van Aken, eds. M.I.T. Symposium on American Women in Science and Engineering, 1964. Women and the Scientific Professions (Cambridge, MA: M.I.T. Press, 1965)

1047. Meisol, Patricia. "Women in Politics-- Increasing in Numbers, But Not on the Hill," National Journal, Vol. 10 (July 1968), pp. 1128-1131

1048. Merritt, Sharyne. "Winners and Losers: Sex Differences in Municipal Elections," American Journal of Political Science, Vol. 21 (November 1977), pp. 731-743

1049. Messinger, Ruth. "Women in Power and Politics," The Future of Difference, Eisenstein, Hester and Alice Jardine, eds. (Boston: G. K. Hall, 1980), pp. 318-326

1050. Mezey, Susan Gluck. "Does Sex Make A Difference?: A Case Study of Women in Politics," Western Political Quarterly, Vol. 31 (December 1978), pp. 492-501

1051. Mezey, Susan Gluck. "Women and Representation: The Case of Hawaii," Journal of Politics, Vol. 40 (May 1978), pp. 369-385

1052. Mullins, Carolyn. "The Plight of the Board-woman: The Female Schoolboard Member Still Has a Tough Time Of It, This Study Shows, But Her Number Is Growing--and So Is Her Determination," American School Board Journal, Vol. 159 (February 1972), pp. 27-32

1053. National Women's Education Fund. Facts: Women and Public Life (Washington, DC, 1975)

1054. Ness, Susan and Frederick Wechsler. "Woman Judges--Why So Few?" Graduate Woman, Vol. 73 (November-December, 1979), pp. 10-12ff

1055. Neuse, Stephen M. "Sex Employment Patterns in State Government: A Case Study," State Government, Vol. 52 (Spring 1979), pp. 52-57

1056. Neuse, Stephen M. "Professionalism and Authority: Women in Public Service," Public Administration Review, Vol. 38 (September 1978), pp. 436-441

1057. Okanes, M. M. and L. W. Murray. "Achievement and Machiavellianism Among Men and Women Managers," Psychological Report, Vol. 46 (June 1980), pp. 783-788

1058. Pastor, J. "Hispanic Female in City Management," Public Management, Vol. 62 (October 1980), pp. 20-21

1059. Perkins, Jerry and Diane L. Fowlkes. "Opinion Representation vs. Social Representation, or, Why Women Can't Run as Women and Win," The American Political Science Review, Vol. 74 (March 1980), pp. 92-103

1060. Porter, Mary C. and Ann B. Matasar. "The Role and Status of Women in the Daley Organization," Women in Politics, Jaquette, Jane S., ed. (New York: Wiley, 1974), pp. 85-109

1061. Powell, L. W. et al. "Male and Female Differences in Elite Political Participation: An Examination of the Effects of Socioeconomic and Familial Variables," Western Political Quarterly, Vol. 34 (March 1981), pp. 31-45

1062. Radin, Beryl A. International Women's Year Conference on Women in Public Life. Women in Public Life: Report of a Conference, Co-Sponsored by the Lyndon Baines Johnson Library and the Lyndon B. Johnson School of Public Affairs (Austin, Texas, November 9-11, 1975) (Austin, TX: Lyndon B. Johnson School of Public Affairs, University of Texas, 1976)

1063. Rosen, Benson. "The First Few Years on the Job:
      Women in Management; Women Go Into Management
      for the Same Reasons that Men Do, But Have Some
      Special Difficulties Once They Get There
      (Results of a 1979 Survey of Female and Male
      MBAs)," Business Horizons, Vol. 24
      (November-December, 1981), pp. 26-29

1064. Ruddick, Sara and Pamela Daniels. Working It
      Out: 23 Women Writers, Artists, Scientists, and
      Scholars Talk About Their Lives and Work (New
      York: Pantheon Books, 1978)

1065. Rule, W. "Why Women Don't Run: The Critical
      Contextual Factors in Women's Legislative
      Recruitment," Western Political Quarterly, Vol.
      34 (March 1981), pp. 60-77

1066. Scanlan, M. "Women in Local Government
      Management," Public Management, Vol. 61 (May
      1979), pp. 17-18

1067. Schramm, Sarah Slavin. "Women and
      Representation: Self-Government and Role
      Changes," Western Political Quarterly, Vol. 34
      (March 1981), pp. 46-59

1068. Schreiber, F. M. "Education and Change in
      American Opinions on a Woman for President,"
      Public Opinion Quarterly, Vol. 42 (Summer 1978),
      pp. 171-182

1069. Scott, M. Gladys and Mary J. Hoferek. Women as
      Leaders in Physical Education and Sports (Iowa
      City, IA: University of Iowa Press, 1979)

1070. Stewart, Debra W., ed. Women in Local Politics
      (Metuchen, NJ: Scarecrow Press, 1980)

1071. Stewart, Debra W. The Women's Movement in
      Community Politics in the U.S.: The Role of
      Local Commissions on the Status of Women (New
      York: Pergamon Press, 1980)

1072. Stewart, Nathaniel. The Effective Woman
      Manager: Seven Vital Skills for Upward Mobility
      (New York: Ballantine Books, 1978)

1073. Stoper, Emily. "Wife and Politician: Role
      Strain Among Women in Public Office," A Portrait
      of Marginality: The Political Behavior of the
      American Woman, Githens, Marianne and Jewel L.
      Prestage, eds. (New York: David McKay Co.,
      1977), pp. 320-338

1074. Sweet, Ellen. "The New Congresswoman," Ms.,
      Vol. 9 (February 1981), p. 102

1075. Thompsons, J. H. "Role Perceptions of Women in
      the Ninety-Fourth Congress: 1975-1976,"
      Political Science Quarterly, Vol. 95 (Spring
      1980), pp. 71-81

1076. Tolchin, Susan and Martin Tolchin. Clout:
      Womanpower and Politics (New York: Coward,
      McCann & Geoghegan, 1974)

1077. Vaden, Richard E. and Naomi B. Lynn. "The
      Administrative Person: Will Women Bring a
      Differing Morality to Management," University of
      Michigan Business Review, Vol. 31 (March 1979),
      pp. 22-25

1078. Van Hightowern, Nikki R. "The Recruitment of
      Women for Public Office," American Politics
      Quarterly, Vol. 5 (July 1977), pp. 301-314

1079. Welch, Susan and Albert K. Kamig. "Correlates
      of Female Office Holding in City Politics," The
      Journal of Politics, Vol. 41 (May 1979), pp.
      478-491

1080. Wells, Audrey S. and Eleanor C. Smeal. "Women's
      Attitudes Toward Women in Politics: A Survey of
      Urban Registered Voters and Party Committee
      Women," Women in Politics, Jaquette, Jane S.,
      ed. (New York: Wiley, 1974), pp. 54-72

1081. Welsh, M. C. "Attitudinal Measures and
      Evaluation of Males and Females in Leadership
      Roles," Psychological Report, Vol. 45 (August
      1979), pp. 19-22

1082. Werner, Emmy. "Women in State Legislatures,"
      Western Political Quarterly, Vol. 21 (March
      1968), pp. 40-50

1083. Werner, Emmy. "Women in Congress: 1917-1964,"
      Western Political Quarterly, Vol. 19 (March
      1966), pp. 17-30

1084. Werner, Emmy E. and Louise M. Bachtold.
      "Personality Characteristics of Women in
      American Politics," Women in Politics, Jaquette,
      Jane S., ed. (New York: Wiley, 1974), pp. 75-85

1085. "Why Aren't There More Women in Congress?"
      Congressional Quarterly Weekly Report, Vol. 36
      (August 12, 1978), pp. 2108-2110

1086. "Women Candidates: Many More Predicted for
      1974," Congressional Quarterly Weekly Report,
      Vol. 32 (April 13, 1974), pp. 941-944

1087. "Women in Local Government Management," Public
      Management, Vol. 61 (May 1979), pp. 17-18

1088. "Women in Politics: Leading Candidates in 1970,
      Their Election Prospects, Past and Present
      Members (of the Congress)," Congressional
      Quarterly Weekly Report, Vol. 28 (July 10,
      1970), pp. 1745-1748

1089. Women in Public Office: A Biographical
      Directory and Statistical Analyses (Metuchen,
      NJ: Scarecrow Press, 1980)

1090. "The Women Who Serve on Boards [lists the 324
      women serving on the boards of the top 1300

financial, retail and service firms; U.S.],"
Business and Society Review, (Spring 1980-1981),
pp. 25-30

XI. SOCIAL POLICY IN AMERICA

1091. Abramson, Joan. Old Boys, New Women: The Politics of Sex Discrimination (New York: Praeger Publishers, 1979)

1092. Adams, Carolyn Teich and Kathryn Teich Winston. Mothers at Work: Public Policies in the U.S., Sweden and China (New York: Longman, 1980)

1093. Baer, Judith A. The Chains of Protection: The Judicial Response to Women's Labor Legislation (Westport, CT: Greenwood Press, 1978)

1094. Becker, Gary S. A Treatise on the Family (Cambridge, MA: Harvard University Press, 1981)

1095. Bellamy, C. "Rethinking Public Policy for Families," Human Ecology Forum, Vol. 10 (Spring 1980), pp. 3-6

1096. Berger, Brigitte and Sidney Callahan, eds. Child Care and Mediating Structures, (Washington, DC: American Enterprise Institute, 1976)

1097. Berlow, Albert. "Constitutional Law Experts Disagree Over Extension of ERA Approval Deadline," Congressional Quarterly Weekly Report, Vol. 35 (November 26, 1977), pp. 2493-2496

133

1098. Bernard, Jessie. "Women and New Social
      Systems," The American Woman: Who Will She Be?,
      McBee, Mary Louise and Kathryn A. Blake, eds.
      (Beverly Hills, CA: Glencoe, 1974), pp. 81-93

1099. Bessmer, S. "Anti-obscenity: A Comparison of
      the Legal and the Feminist Perspectives,"
      Western Political Quarterly, Vol. 34 (March
      1981), pp. 143-155

1100. Binkin, Martin and Shirley Bach. Women and the
      Military (Washington, DC: The Brookings
      Institution, 1977)

1101. Blau, Francine D. and Lawrence M. Kahn. "Causes
      and Consequences of Layoffs (comparison of
      effects on blacks, whites and women; U.S.),"
      Economic Inquiry, Vol. 19 (April 1981), pp.
      270-296

1102. Boles, Janet K. The Politics of the Equal
      Rights Amendment: Conflict and the Decision
      Process (New York: Longman, 1979)

1103. Boneparth, Ellen, ed. Women, Power and Policy
      (New York: Pergamon Press, 1982)

1104. Bradbury, Katherine. "Public Assistance, Female
      Headship, and Economic Well-Being," Journal of
      Marriage and the Family, Vol. 41 (August 1979),
      pp. 519-35

1105. Brown, Barbara A; Ann E. Freedman; Harriet N.
      Katz; and Alice M. Price. Women's Rights and
      the Law: The Impact of the ERA on State Laws
      (New York: Praeger, 1977)

1106. Brown, Barbara A. et al. "The Equal Rights
      Amendment: A Constitutional Basis for Equal
      Rights for Women," Yale Law Journal, Vol. 80
      (April 1971), pp. 871-895

1107. Buchanan, Christopher. "Extension Asked for
      Equal Rights Amendment," Congressional Quarterly
      Weekly Report, Vol. 35 (November 5, 1977), pp.
      2369-2370

1108. Burstein, P. and M. W. MacLeod. "Prohibiting
      Employment Discrimination: Ideas and Politics
      in the Congressional Debate Over Equal
      Opportunity Legislation," American Journal of
      Sociology, Vol. 86 (November 1980), pp. 512-533

1109. California Commission on the Status of Women.
      Impact ERA: Limitations and Possibilities
      (Milbrae, CA: Les Femmes Publishing, 1976)

1110. Callahan, D. "Abortion and Government Policy,"
      Family Planning Perspectives, Vol. 11
      (September-October 1979), pp. 275-282

1111. Calvani, Terry. "Homosexuality and the Law--An
      Overview," New York Law Forum, Vol. 17, (1971),
      pp. 272-303

1112. Cates, W. et al. "Health Impact of Restricting
      Public Funds for Abortion, October 10, 1977-June
      10, 1978," American Journal of Public Health,
      Vol. 69 (Spring 1979), pp. 945-947

1113. Cates, Willard, Jr. "Legal Abortion: Are
      American Black Women Healthier Because of It?"
      Phylon, Vol. 38 (September 1977), pp. 267-281

1114. Cech, Barbara. "Policy and Planning in the Drug
      Abuse Field," Frontiers, Vol. 4 (Summer 1979),
      pp. 1-4

1115. Chaddock, Paul. Sexual Harassment (Princeton,
      NJ: Petrocelli Books, Inc., 1981)

1116. Chandler, Melinda P. "Equal Pay for Comparable
      Work Value: The Failure of Title VII (of the
      Civil Rights Act of 1964) and the Equal Pay

136   AMERICAN WOMEN AND POLITICS

Act," <u>Northwestern University Law Review</u>, Vol.
75 (December 1980), pp. 914-943

1117. Chilman, Catherine. "Public Social Policy and
Families in the 1970s," <u>Social Casework</u>, Vol. 54
(December 1973), pp. 575-585

1118. Christie, Claudia M. "Who's Watching the
Children? The Cost and Availability of Day Care
Facilities are Crucial Issues to Women Who
Work—And to Companies That Want to Welcome
Women to Their Workforce," <u>New England Business</u>,
Vol. 3 (October 5, 1981), pp. 21-23

1119. Cohodas, Nadine. "The Elusive Three States:
With Only Two Years To Go, ERA (Equal Rights
Amendment) Still Faces an Uphill Fight and Murky
Legal Questions," <u>Congressional Quarterly Weekly
Report</u>, Vol. 38 (June 28, 1980), pp. 1813-1815

1120. "The Continuing Controversy Over the Women's
Equal Rights Amendment: Pro and Con,"
<u>Congressional Digest</u>, Vol. 56 (June-July 1977),
pp. 162-192

1121. Crothers, Diane. "The AT&T Settlement," <u>Women's
Rights Law Reporter</u>, Vol. 1 (Summer 1973), pp.
5-13

1122. David, Henry P. et al (eds). <u>Abortion in
Psychosexual Perspective: Trends in Trans-
national Research</u> (New York: Springer, 1978)

1123. DeCrow, Karen. <u>Sexist Justice</u> (New York:
Vintage Books, 1975)

1124. Denmark, Florence, ed. <u>Who Discriminates
Against Women?</u> (Beverly Hills, CA: Sage
Publications, 1974)

1125. Dinerman, Miriam. "Catch 23: Women, Work, and
Welfare," <u>Social Work</u>, Vol. 22 (November 1977),

pp. 472-477, and "Author Responds," Social Work, Vol. 23 (May 1978), pp. 263-264

1126. Donnison, David. "Feminism's Second Wave and Supplementary Benefits," Political Quarterly, Vol. 49 (July 1978), pp. 271-284

1127. Dreifus, Claudia, ed. Seizing Our Bodies: The Politics of Women's Health Care (New York: Vintage Books, 1978)

1128. Ellis, Judy Trent. "Sexual Harassment and Race: a Legal Analysis of Discrimination," Journal of Legislation, Vol. 8 (Winter 1981), pp. 30-45

1129. Epstein, Cynthia Fuchs, ed. The Other Half: Roads to Women's Equality (Englewood Cliffs, NJ: Prentice-Hall, 1971)

1130. "Equal Pay for Comparable Work (argues that sex discrimination has depressed compensation levels for jobs filled primarily by women, just as it has reduced pay in sexually integrated jobs)," Harvard Civil Rights-Civil Liberties Law Review, Vol. 15 (Fall 1980), pp. 475-506

1131. "Equal Rights Amendment: Amendment Passed Over Ervin Opposition (H.J. res. 208, approved by the Senate, March 22, 1972, and sent to the states for ratification)," Congressional Quarterly Weekly Report, Vol. 30 (March 25, 1972), pp. 692-695

1132. Erickson, Nancy S. "Pregnancy Discrimination: An Analytical Approach," Women's Rights Law Reporter, Vol. 5 (Winter-Spring 1979), pp. 83-105

1133. "Family Policy Research," Journal of Marriage and the Family, Vol. 40 (August 1978), Special Issue

1134. Fierst, Edith U. "Why Congress Zapped Pensions
      for Women: A Half A Million Women Unknowingly
      are Donating Their Tax-Deferred Pensions to
      Their More Affluent Bosses; When the Internal
      Revenue Service Tried to Do Something About It,
      Congress Said 'No'; Here's Why--and a Chance to
      Turn Congress Around," Graduate Woman, Vol. 75
      (November-December 1981), pp. 16-18

1135. Flowers, Marilyn R. Women and Social Security:
      An Institutional Dilemma (Washington, DC:
      American Enterprise Institute, 1979)

1136. Forrest, J. D.; E. Sullivan; and C. Tietzu.
      "Abortion in the U.S. 1977-78," Family Planning
      Perspectives, Vol. 11 (November-December 1979),
      pp. 329-341

1137. France, Judith E. and Michael C. Seeborg.
      "Labor Market Performance of Female CETA
      Participants," Economic Forum, Vol. 10 (Summer
      1979), pp. 55-64

1138. Francome, C. "Abortion Policy in Britain and
      the U.S.," Social Work, Vol. 25 (January 1980),
      pp.5-11

1139. Gelb, Joyce and Marian Lief Palley. Women and
      Public Policies (Princeton, NJ: Princeton
      University Press, 1982)

1140. Gertner, Nancy. "Bakke on Affirmative Action
      for Women: Pedestal or Cage," Harvard Civil
      Rights-Civil Liberties Law Review, Vol. 14
      (Spring 1979), pp. 173-214

1141. Giele, Janet Zollinger. "Family Policy," in her
      Women and the Future: Changing Sex Roles in
      Modern America (New York: The Free Press,
      1978), pp. 188-242

1142. Ginsberg, Ruth Bader. "Sex Equality and the
      Constitution: The State of the Art

(Constitutional Bases for Legal Suits)," Women's Rights Law Reporter, Vol. 4 (Spring 1978), pp. 143-147

1143. Ginsberg, Ruth Bader. "Women, Equality and the Bakke Case (How the Supreme Court Has Treated Affirmative Action for Women)," Civil Liberties Review, Vol. 4 (November-December 1977), pp. 8-16

1144. Giraldo, Z. I. Public Policy and the Family: Wives and Mothers in the Labor Force (Lexington, MA: Lexington Books 1980)

1145. Goldman, Jane. "Unions, Women and Economic Justice: Litigating Union Sex Discrimination," Women's Rights Law Reporter, Vol. 4 (Fall 1977), pp. 3-26

1146. Goldman, Nancy Loring, ed. Female Soldiers-- Combatants or Non-Combatants?: Historical and Contemporary Perspectives (Westport, CT: Greenwood Press, 1982)

1147. Goldstein, Leslie Friedman. "The Constitutional Status of Women: The Burger Court and Sexual Revolution in American Law," Law and Policy Quarterly, Vol. 3 (January 1981), pp. 5-28

1148. Goodman, Jill Laurie. "Women, War, and Equality: An Examination of Sex Discrimination in the Military," Women's Rights Law Reporter, Vol. 5 (Summer 1979), pp. 243-269

1149. Grad, Susan. "Impact on Widows of Proposed Changes in OASI (Old-Age and Survivors Insurance) Mother's Benefits (Impact of a proposal that would terminate mother's and father's benefits when the young child in care of the surviving spouse reaches age 16, rather than age 18, as in current law)," Social Security Bulletin, Vol. 44 (February 1981), pp. 3-18

1150. Gross, Barry R. Discrimination in Reverse: Is
      Turnabout Fair Play (New York: New York
      University Press, 1978)

1151. Hamermesh, D. S. "Entitlement Effects
      Unemployed Insurance and Employment Decisions,"
      Economic Inquiry, Vol. 17 (July 1979), pp.
      317-332

1152. Hill, Ann Corinne. "Protection of Women Workers
      and the Courts: A Legal Case History," Feminist
      Studies, Vol. 5 (Summer 1979), pp. 247-273

1153. Hofferth, Sandra L. "Day Care in the Next
      Decade: 1980-1990," Journal of Marriage and the
      Family, Vol. 41 (August 1979), pp. 649-658

1154. Hogan, Betsy. "Blacks vs. Women: When Victims
      Collide; Minorities and Women Compete for
      Employment Gains; They Should Form a Cartel to
      Enlarge the Gains," Business and Society
      Review/Innovation, No. 10 (Summer 1974), pp.
      71-77

1155. Hughes, Marija Matich. The Sexual Barrier:
      Legal, Medical, Economic and Social Aspects of
      Sex Discrimination (Washington, DC: Hughes
      Press, 1977)

1156. Hutchens, R. M. "Entry and Exit Transitions in
      a Government Transfer Program: The Case of Aid
      to Families with Dependent Children," Journal of
      Human Resources, Vol. 16 (Spring 1981), pp.
      217-237

1157. Jacobs, Roger B. "The Manhart Case: Sex-Based
      Differentials and the Application of Title VII
      to Pensions," Labor Law Journal, Vol. 31 (April
      1980), pp. 232-246

1158. Jacobson, Carolyn J. "ERA: Ratifying
      Equality," American Federationist, Vol. 82
      (January 1975), pp. 9-13

1159. Jarrard, Mary W. "Emerging ERA Patterns in Editorials in Southern Daily Newspapers: Conservative Rhetoric Evident in Editorials in Newspapers from 1970 to 1977," Journalism Quarterly, Vol. 57 (Winter 1980), pp. 606-611

1160. Johnson, Carolyn. "Women and Retirement: A Study and Implications," Family Relations, Vol. 29 (June 1980), pp. 380-385

1161. Kamerman, Sheila B. and Alfred J. Kahn. Child Care, Family Benefits, and Working Parents: A Study in Comparative Policy (New York: Columbia University Press, 1981)

1162. Kamerman, Sheila B. and Alfred J. Kahn. "Day-Care Debate: A Wider View," Public Interest, Vol. 54 (Winter 1979), pp. 76-93

1163. Kamerman, Sheila B. and Alfred J. Kahn, eds. Family Policy: Government and Families in 14 Countries (New York: Columbia University Press, 1978)

1164. Karg, Bernice. "Restrictions on Women's Right to Abortion: Informed Consent, Spousal Consent, and Recordkeeping Provisions," Women's Rights Law Reporter, Vol. 5 (Fall 1978), pp. 35-51

1165. Kirschten, Dick. "Reagan's approach to women's issues -- let them simmer on the back burner: the President has appointed few women to top posts in his administration, and he has been slow to support legislative proposals to eliminate sex discrimination," National Journal, Vol. 13 (May 23, 1981), pp. 926-27

1166. Kitchen, Brigitte. "The Family and the State," International Journal of Women's Studies, Vol. 4 (March-April 1981), pp. 181-195

1167. Leepson, Marc. "Affirmative Action Recon-
       sidered," Editorial Research Reports, Vol. II
       (July 31, 1981), pp. 553-572

1168. Lester, Richard A. Reasoning About Discrimi-
       nation: The Analysis of Professional and
       Executive Work in Federal Antibias Programs
       (Princeton, NJ: Princeton University Press,
       1980)

1169. Levine, James A. et al. for the United States
       Commission on Civil Rights. Child Care and Equal
       Opportunity for Women (Washington, DC: U.S.
       Government Printing Office, June 1981)

1170. Levy, Frank. "The Labor Supply of Female
       Household Heads, or AFDC Incentives Don't Work
       Too Well," Journal of Human Resources, Vol. 14
       (Winter 1979), pp. 76-79

1171. Lindheim, B. L. "Services, Policies and Costs
       in U.S. Abortion Facilities," Family Planning
       Perspectives, Vol. 11 (September-October 1979),
       pp.283-288

1172. Lipman-Blumen, Jean and Jessie S. Bernard, eds.
       Sex Roles and Social Policy: A Complex Social
       Science Equation (Beverly Hills, CA: Sage,
       1979)

1173. Loewy, Arnold H. "Returned to the Pedestal--The
       Supreme Court and Gender Classification Cases:
       1980 Term," North Carolina Law Review, Vol. 60
       (October 1981), pp. 87-101

1174. Malkiel, Burton G. and Judith A. Malkiel.
       "Male-Female Pay Differentials in Professional
       Employment," American Economic Review, Vol. 63
       (September 1973), pp. 693-705

1175. Markson, Elizabeth W., ed. Older Women: Issues
       and Prospects (Lexington, MA: Lexington Books,
       1983)

1176. Martin, Gerald C. "Gender Discrimination in
      Pension Plans Revisited: The Results of Court
      Ordered Implementation," Journal of Risk and
      Insurance, Vol. 46 (December 1979), pp. 727-732

1177. Morgan, James N. et al. Five Thousand American
      Families--Patterns of Economic Process, Vols.
      1-9 (Ann Arbor, MI: Survey Research Center,
      Institute for Social Research, University of
      Michigan, Vol. 1, 1974; Vol. 9, 1981)

1178. Moroney, R. M. The Family and the State:
      Considerations for Social Policy (London:
      Longman Group Limited, 1976)

1179. Murphy, Irene L. Public Policy on the Status of
      Women: Agenda and Strategy for the 1970s
      (Lexington, MA: D. C. Heath, 1973)

1180. Nannes, Margaret for the United States
      Department of State: United States Women:
      Issues and Progress in the U.N. Decade for
      Women, 1976-1985. (Washington, DC: U.S.
      Government Printing Office, September 1980)

1181. Nichols, Abigail C. "Why Welfare Mothers Work:
      Implications for Employment and Training
      Services," Social Service Review, Vol. 533
      (Spring 1979), pp. 378-391

1182. O'Brien, Mary. The Politics of Reproduction
      (Boston: Routledge and Kegan Paul, 1981)

1183. Ogden, Warren C., Jr. "Justice and the Problem
      of the Volitional Victim (Commenting on efforts
      to extend antidiscrimination laws passed to
      protect women, blacks, and other minorities to
      alcoholics, drug addicts, the obese and
      homosexuals)," Labor Law Journal, Vol. 28 (July
      1977), pp. 417-420

1184. O'Kelly, Charlotte G. "The Impact of Equal
      Employment Legislation on Women's Earnings:

Limitations of Legislative Solutions to
Discrimination in the Economy (United States),"
American Journal of Economics and Sociology,
Vol. 38 (October 1979), pp. 419-430

1185. Palley, Marian Lief and Michael B. Preston, eds.
Race, Sex, and Policy Problems (Lexington, MA:
D. C. Heath and Company, 1979)

1186. Petchesky, Rosalind. "Workers, Reproductive
Hazards, and the Politics of Protection: An
Introduction," Feminist Studies, Vol. 5 (Summer
1979), pp. 233-245

1187. Peterson, Samiha S; Judy M. Richardson; and
Gretchen V. Kreuter, eds. The Two-Career
Family: Issues and Alternatives (Washington,
DC: University Press of America, 1978)

1188. Plannel, Raymond M. "The Equal Rights
Amendment: Will States be Allowed to Change
Their Minds?," Notre Dame Lawyer, Vol. 49
(February 1974), pp. 657-670

1189. Proxmire, William and John K. Singlaub. "Should
Women be Used in Military Combat? Opposing
Views on a Question," American Legion Magazine,
Vol. 105 (September 1978), pp. 30-31

1190. "Public Support for ERA Reaches New High,"
Gallup Report, No. 190 (July 1981), pp. 23-25

1191. "Quotas (or is it goals?) Condemned by Both
Sides (debate over whether the federal
government should require mandatory employment
percentages for minorities and women),"
Congressional Quarterly Weekly Report, Vol. 30
(December 2, 1972), pp. 3092-3093

1192. Rainwater, Lee. "Notes on U. S. Family Policy,"
Social Policy, Vol. 8 (March 1978), pp. 28-30

1193. "Ratification Facts and Figures (Information on
      the states that have and have not ratified the
      Equal Rights Amendment)," Graduate Woman, Vol.
      74 (March-April 1980), pp. 12-13

1194. Rein, Martin and Lee Rainwater. "Patterns of
      Welfare Use," Social Service Review, Vol. 52
      (December 1978), pp. 511-524

1195. "Research on the Violations of Civil Liberties
      of Homosexual Men and Women," Journal of
      Homosexuality, Vol. 2 (Summer 1977), pp. 313-342

1196. "Restructuring the Social Security System (to
      reflect changing status of women in terms of
      marriage, divorce and employment)," CLU
      (Chartered Life Underwriters) Journal, Vol. 35
      (April 1981), pp. 38-43

1197. Robins, P. K. et al. "Effects of SIME/DIME on
      Changes in Employment Status," Journal of Human
      Resources, Vol. 15 (Fall 1980), pp. 545-573

1198. Rogge, John O. "Equal Rights for Women
      (Historical Analysis of the Body of Litigation
      Involving the Rights of Women)," Harvard Law
      Journal, Vol. 21 (November 2, 1978), pp. 327-420

1199. Rose, Vicki McNickle. "Rape as a Social
      Problem: A Byproduct of the Feminist Movement,"
      Social Problems, Vol. 25 (October 1977), pp.
      78-89

1200. Rosenman, Linda S. "Unemployment of Women: A
      Social Policy Issue," Social Work Vol. 24
      (January 1979), pp. 20-25

1201. Ross, Heather L. and Isabel V. Sawhill. Time of
      Transition: The Growth of Families Headed by
      Women (Washington, DC: The Urban Institute,
      1975)

1202. Rubin, C. L. "Response of Low Income Women and
      Abortion Facilities to Restriction of Public
      Funds for Abortion: A Study of a Large
      Metropolitan Area," American Journal of Public
      Health, Vol. 69 (Spring 1979), pp. 948-949

1203. Safilos-Rothschild, Constantina. Women and
      Social Policy (Englewood Cliffs, NJ:
      Prentice-Hall, 1974)

1204. Sawhill, Isabel V. "The Economics of
      Discrimination Against Women: Some New
      Findings," Journal of Human Resources, Vol. 8
      (Summer 1973), pp. 383-396

1205. Schaffer, Helen B. "Child Support," Editorial
      Research Reports on the Women's Movement
      (Washington, DC: Congressional Quarterly, Inc.
      1977), pp. 143-163

1206. Schorr, Alvin L. "Single Parents, Women, and
      Public Policy," Institute of Socioeconomic
      Studies Journal, Vol. 6 (Winter 1981-1982), pp.
      100-113

1207. "'Sexist' Social Security Under Attack: Working
      Wives, Homemakers and Divorced Women Say They've
      Been Short-changed by the Retirement System; the
      Problem: Can the Shaky Pension Setup Afford to
      be More Generous?" U.S. News, Vol. 84 (May 29,
      1978), pp. 81-82

1208. Shariff, Zahid. "Intra-Family Equality and
      Income Distribution: Emerging Conflicts in
      Public Policy," American Journal of Economics
      and Sociology, Vol. 38 (January 1979), pp. 49-59

1209. Simpson, Peg. "A Victory for Women: The New
      Pregnancy Disability Law Reverses the Supreme
      Court," Civil Rights Digest, Vol. 11 (Spring
      1979), pp. 12-21

1210. Simpson, Ruth. From the Closets to the Courts
      (New York: Penguin, 1976)

1211. Singer, James W. "Undervalued Jobs--What's a
      Woman (and the Government) to Do? The Equal
      Employment Opportunity Commission is Considering
      Regulations Against a Subtle Form of
      Discrimination: Low Wages for Jobs held Mostly
      by Women," National Journal, Vol. 12 (May 24,
      1980), pp. 858-862

1212. Smedley, Larry. "Maintaining the Balance in
      Social Security (Financing Problems, Relation to
      Private Pension Plans, Retirement Provision and
      Women in the System)," American Federationist,
      Vol. 86 (February 1979), pp. 20-25

1213. Smith, Ralph E., ed. The Subtle Revolution:
      Women at Work (Washington, DC: The Urban
      Institute, 1979). Particularly Nancy M. Gordon,
      "Institutional Responses: The Federal Income
      Tax System," "Institutional Responses: The
      Social Security System," pp. 201-257

1214. Sowell, Thomas. Affirmative Action
      Reconsidered: Was it Necessary in Academia?
      (Washington, DC: American Enterprise Institute,
      1975)

1215. Spritzer, Allen D. "Equal Employment
      Opportunity Versus Protection for Women: A
      Public Policy Dilemma (United States)," Alabama
      Law Review, Vol. 24 (Summer 1972), pp. 567-606

1216. Stanley-Elliott, Lynne E. "Sexual Harassment in
      the Workplace: Title VII's Imperfect Relief,"
      Journal of Corporate Law, Vol. 6 (Spring 1981),
      pp. 625-656

1217. Staples, Robert. "Public Policy and Changing
      Status of the Black Family," Family Coordinator,
      Vol. 22 (June 1973), pp. 345-352

1218. Steinberg, Larry. "The Long Haul for ERA and
      Now, Division in the Ranks: Supporters of the
      Equal Rights Amendment are Divided Over the
      Wisdom of Seeking an Extension of the
      Ratification Deadline," National Journal, Vol. 9
      (December 31, 1977), pp. 2006-2008

1219. Steiner, Gilbert Y. The Futility of Family
      Policy (Washington, DC: Brookings Institution,
      1981)

1220. Suphan, Andic. "Does the Personal Income Tax
      Discriminate Against Women?," Public Finance
      Vol. 36, No 1 (1981), pp. 1-15

1221. Taylor, Ellen T. "Differential Treatment of
      Pregnancy in Employment: The Impact of General
      Electric Co. v. Gilbert and Nashville Gas Co. v.
      Satty," Harvard Civil Rights—Civil Liberties
      Law Review, Vol. 13 (Summer 1978), pp. 717-750

1222. United States Commission on Civil Rights.
      Social Indicators of Equality for Minorities and
      Women (Washington, DC: Government Printing
      Office, August 1978)

1223. United States Commission on Civil Rights.
      Statement on the Equal Rights Amendment
      (Washington, DC: U.S. Government Printing
      Office, December 1978)

1224. United States Congress, House of Representa-
      tives, Committee on Armed Services, Military
      Personnel Subcommittee. Registration of Women:
      Hearing on H.R. 6569, 96th Congress, 2nd
      Session, March 5-6, 1980 (Washington, DC: U.S.
      Government Printing Office 1980)

1225. United States Congress, House of Representa-
      tives, Committee on Education and Labor,
      Subcommittee on Employment Opportunities.
      Legislation to Prohibit Sex Discrimination on
      the Basis of Pregnancy: Hearing on H.R. 5055

and H.R. 6075, to Amend Title VII of the Civil
Rights Act of 1964, 95th Congress, 1st Session;
April 6, 1977 (Washington, DC: U.S. Government
Printing Office, 1977)

1226. United States Congress, House of Representa-
tives, Committee on the Judiciary, Subcommittee
No. 4. Equal Rights for Men and Women 1971:
Hearings on H. J. res. 35 [and] 208 and Related
Bills and H. R. 916 and Related Bills. 92nd
Congress, 1st Session, March 24-April 5, 1971
(Washington, DC: U.S. Government Printing
Office, 1971)

1227. United States Congress, House of Representatives, Committee on the Judiciary, Subcommittee
on Civil and Constitutional Rights. Equal
Rights Amendment Extension: Hearings on H. J.
Res. 638, Extending the Ratification Period for
the Proposed Equal Rights Amendment, 95th
Congress, 1st and 2nd Sessions, November 1,
1977-May 19, 1978 (Washington, DC: U.S.
Government Printing Office, 1978)

1228. United States Congress, House of Representatives, Committee on Ways and Means, Subcommittee
on Social Security. Hearings on the Treatment
of Men and Women Under the Social Security
program, 96th Congress, 1st Session, November
1-2, 1979 (Washington, DC: U.S. Government
Printing Office, 1980)

1229. United States Congress, House of Representa-
tives, Select Committee on Aging, Subcommittee
on Retirement, Income and Employment. Women and
Retirement Income Programs: Current Issues of
Equality and Adequacy: A Report, November, 1979
(Washington, DC: U.S. Government Printing
Office, 1979)

1230. United States Congress, House of Representatives, Committee on Education and Labor,
Subcommittee on Employment Opportunities. Civil

150   AMERICAN WOMEN AND POLITICS

Rights Amendments Act of 1979: Hearing on H.R.
2074, to Prohibit Discrimination on the Basis of
Affectional or Sexual Orientation, and for Other
Purposes, 96th Congress, 2nd Session, October
10, 1980 (Washington, DC: U.S. Government
Printing Office, 1980)

1231. United States Congress, Senate, Committee on
Human Resources, Subcommittee on Child and Human
Development. Domestic Violence, 1978: Hearings
on Domestic Violence and Legislation with
Respect to Domestic Violence, 95th Congress, 2nd
Session, March 4, 8, 1978 (Washington, DC: U.S.
Government Printing Office, 1978)

1232. United States Congress, Senate, Committee on
Labor and Human Resources, Subcommittee on Child
and Human Development. Domestic Violence
Prevention and Services Act, 1980: hearing on
S. 1843, 96th Congress, 2nd Session, February 6,
1980 (Washington, DC: U.S. Government Printing
Office, 1980)

1233. United States Congress, Senate, Committee on the
Judiciary. Equal Rights 1970: Hearings on S.J.
res. 61 and S.J. res. 231, 91st Congress, 2nd
Session, September 9-15, 1970 (Washington, DC:
U.S. Government Printing Office, 1970)

1234. United States Congress, Senate, Committee on the
Judiciary, Subcommittee on Constitutional
Amendments. The "Equal Rights" Amendment:
Hearings on S.J. res 61, 91st Congress, 2nd
Session, May 5-7, 1970 (Washington, DC: U.S.
Government Printing Office, 1970)

1235. United States Congress, Senate, Committee of the
Judiciary, Subcommittee on the Constitution.
Equal Rights Amendment Extension: Hearings on
S.J. Res. 134, Joint Resolution Extending the
Deadline for the Ratification of the Equal
Rights Amendment, 95th Congress, 2nd Session,

August 2-4, 1978 (Washington, DC: U.S.
Government Printing Office, 1979)

1236. United States Congress, Senate, Special
Committee on Aging. Impact of Federal Estate
Tax Policies on Rural Women: Hearing, 97th
Congress, 1st Session, February 4, 1981
(Washington DC: U. S. Government Printing
Office 1981)

1237. United States Department of Health, Education
and Welfare. Child Care and the Working Woman:
Report and Recommendations of the Secretary's
Advisor Committee on the Rights and
Responsibilities of Women, 1975 (Washington, DC:
U.S. Government Printing Office, 1976)

1238. United States Department of Labor, Women's
Bureau. Native American Women and Equal
Opportunity: How to Get Ahead in the Federal
Government (Washington, DC: U.S. Government
Printing Office, 1979)

1239. United States, Equal Employment Opportunities
Commission. Minorities and Women in Private
Industry: 1978 Report (Washington, DC: U.S.
Government Printing Office, February 1980)

1240. Vercheak, Susan. "State Equal Rights Amendment:
Legislative Reform and Judicial Activism,"
Women's Rights Law Reporter, Vol. 4 (Summer
1978), pp. 227-242

1241. Waite, Linda J. "Changes in Child Care
Arrangments of Working Women from 1965 to 1971,"
Social Science Quarterly, Vol. 58 (September
1977), pp. 302-311

1242. Wattenberg, Esther and Hazel Reinhardt.
"Female-Headed Families: Trends and
Implications," Social Work, Vol. 24 (November
1979), pp. 460-467

1243. Weiss, Laura B. "Women in the Military: Debate
      in House Focuses on Legal Questions, Combat
      Role," Congressional Quarterly Weekly Report,
      Vol. 37 (April 21, 1979), pp. 741-743

1244. Wells, R. V. "Birth Control: Different
      Conceptions," Journal of Interdisciplinary
      History, Vol. 10 (Winter 1980), pp. 511-516

1245. Westoff, Charles F. and Norman B. Ryder. The
      Contraceptive Revolution (Princeton, NJ:
      Princeton University Press, 1977)

1246. Wilson, S. et al. "Guaranteed Employment, Work
      Incentives, and Welfare Reform: Insight From
      the Work Equity Project," American Economic
      Review, Vol. 70 (May 1980), pp. 132-137

1247. Winter, Ralph K., moderator; Qwen Glaser,
      William Raspberry, Paul Seabury, participants.
      Affirmative Action: The Answer to
      Discrimination? (Washington, DC: American
      Enterprise Institute, 1976)

1248. Wise, Donna L. "Challenging Sexual Preference
      Discrimination in Private Employment," Ohio
      State Law Journal, Vol. 41 (November 2, 1980),
      pp. 501-531

1249. Witter, Jean. "Extending Ratification Time for
      the Equal Rights Amendment: Constitionality of
      Time Limitations in the Federal Amending
      Proccess," Women's Rights Law Reporter, Vol. 4
      (Summer 1978), pp. 209-225

1250. Woerness, Kari. "The Invisible Welfare State:
      Women's Work at Home," Acta Sociologica, Vol.
      21, Supplement, (1978), pp. 193-207

1251. Wohl, Lisa Cronin. "White Gloves and Combat
      Boots: The Fight for ERA," Civil Liberties
      Review, Vol. 1 (Fall 1974), pp. 77-86

1252. Wohlenberg, Ernest H. "Correlates of Equal
      Rights Amendment Ratification," Social Science
      Quarterly, Vol. 60 (March 1980), pp. 676-684

1253. Wolgast, Elizabeth H. Equality and the Rights
      of Women (Ithaca, NY: Cornell University Press,
      1980)

1254. "Women and the Draft: The Constitutionality of
      All-Male Registration," Harvard Law Review, Vol.
      94 (December 1980), pp. 406-425

1255. Women Under Attack: Abortion, Sterilization
      Abuse and Reproductive Freedom (New York:
      Committee for Abortion Rights and Against
      Sterilization Abuse, 1979)

1256. Younger, Judith T. "Women's Property Rights Are
      Unfair," Trusts and Estates, Vol. 111 (December
      1972), pp. 942-944

1257. Zashin, Eliot M. "Affirmative Action and Federal
      Personnel Systems," Public Policy, Vol. 28
      (Summer 1980), pp. 351-380

1258. Zurofsky, Bennet D. "Should Minorities and Women
      Be Included in Reverse Discrimination
      Litigation? A Consideration of Federal Rule of
      Civil Procedure 19," Women's Rights Law
      Reporter, Vol. 5 (Winter-Spring 1979), pp.
      165-179

XII. FEMINIST THEORY AND CLASSICAL POLITICAL THEORY
ON THE "WOMAN QUESTION"

1259. Agonito, Rosemary, ed. History of Ideas on
Women (New York: G.P. Putnam's Sons, 1977)

1260. Allen, Christine Garside. "Plato on Women,"
Feminist Studies, Vol. 2 (Feb.-Mar. 1975), pp.
131-138

1261. Annas, Julia. "Mill and the Subjection of
Women," Philosophy, Vol. 52 (April 1977), pp.
179-94

1262. Annas, Julia. "Plato's Republic and Feminism,"
Philosophy, Vol. 51 (July 1976), pp. 307-21

1263. Aristotle. Nichomachean Ethics (Indianapolis,
IN: Bobbs-Merrill Co., 1979)

1264. Aristotle. Politics, Barker, Ernest, ed.
(Oxford: Oxford University Press, 1958)

1265. Arthur, Marilyn. "Early Greece: The Origins of
the Western Attitude Towards Women," Arethusa,
Vol. 6 (Spring 1973), pp. 7-58

1266. Atkinson, Ti-Grace. Amazon Odyssey: The First
Collection of Writings by the Political Pioneer
of the Women's Movement (New York: Quick Fox
Inc., 1974)

1267. Atkinson, Ti-Grace. "Theories of Radical Feminism," Notes from the Second Year: Women's Liberation: Major Writings of the Radical Feminists, Firestone, Shulamith and Anne Koedt, eds., (New York: Radical Feminism, 1970), pp. 32-35

1268. Auerbach, N. "Women on Women's Destiny: Maturity as Penance," Massachusetts Review, Vol. 20 (Summer 1979), pp. 326-334

1269. Balbous, Isaac D. Marxism and Domination: A Neo-Hegelian, Feminist Psychoanalytic Theory of Sexual, Political and Technological Liberation (Princeton, NJ: Princeton University Press, 1982)

1270. Ball, T. "Utilitarianism, Feminism and the Franchise: James Mill and His Critics," The History of Political Thought, Vol. 1 (Spring 1980), pp. 91-116

1271. Barber, Benjamin. Liberating Feminism (New York: Seabury Press, 1975)

1272. Barrett, Michele. Women's Oppression Today: Problems in Marxist Feminist Analysis (New York: Schocken Books, 1981)

1273. Beardsley, Elizabeth Lane. "Referential Genderization," Women and Philosophy, Gould, Carol and Mary Wartofsky, eds., (New York: G. P. Putnam's Sons, 1976), pp. 285-293

1274. de Beauvoir, Simone. The Second Sex, H. M. Parshley trans. and ed. (New York: Knopf, 1953, 1970)

1275. Bebel, August. Woman Under Socialism, De Leon, Daniel, trans. (New York: Schocken Books Inc., 1971)

1276. Benston, Margeret. "The Political Economy of
      Women's Liberation," Monthly Review, Vol. 21,
      (September 1979), pp. 13-27

1277. Birkby, Phyllis, et al., eds. Amazon Expedition
      (Albion, CA: Times Change Press, 1973).

1278. Blackstone, W. and R. Heslepp, eds. Social
      Justice and Preferential Treatment: Women and
      Racial Minorities in Education and Business
      (Athens, GA.: University of Georgia, 1977)

1279. Bouchier, David. "Deradicalisation of Feminism:
      Ideology and Utopia in Action," Sociology, Vol.
      13 (September 1979), pp. 387-402

1280. Boulding, E. "Women and Social Violence,"
      International Social Science Journal, Vol. 30
      (1978), pp. 801-815

1281. Brennan, Teresa and Carole Pateman. "Mere
      Auxiliaries to the Commonwealth: Women and the
      Origins of Liberalism," Political Studies, Vol.
      27 (June 1979), pp. 183-200.

1282. Brooks, Richard A. "Rousseau's Antifeminism in
      the Lettre à d'Alembert and Emile," Literature
      and History in the Age of Ideas, Williams,
      Charles A.S., ed. (Columbus, OH: Ohio State
      University Press, 1975), pp. 209-228

1283. Brownmiller, Susan. Against Our Will: Men,
      Women and Rape (New York: Simon and Schuster,
      1975)

1284. Bunch, Charlotte. "Understanding Feminist
      Theory: Solid Feminist Theory is Basis of Plans
      for Change," New Directions for Women, Vol. 10,
      (September-October 1981), pp. 8-9

1285. Bunch, Charlotte and Nancy Myron, eds. Class
      and Feminism: A Collection of Essays from the
      Furies (Baltimore, MD: Diana Press, 1974)

1286. Burns, Steven. "The Human Female," Dialogue,
      Vol. 15 (September 1976), pp. 415-424

1287. Butler, Melissa. "Early Liberal Roots of
      Feminism: John Locke and the Attack on
      Patriarchy," American Political Science Review,
      Vol. 72 (March 1978), pp. 135-150

1288. Calvert, Brian. "Plato and the Equality of
      Women," Phoenix, Vol. 29 (Autumn 1975) pp.
      231-243

1289. Chapman, Richard Allen. "Leviathan Writ Small:
      Thomas Hobbes on the Family," American Political
      Science Review, Vol. 69 (March 1975) pp. 76-90

1290. Chodorow, Nancy. The Reproduction of Mothering:
      Psychoanalysis and the Sociology of Gender
      (Berkeley, CA: University of California Press,
      1978)

1291. Clark, Lorenne. "The Theory and Practice of the
      Ideology of Male Supremacy," Contemporary Issues
      in Political Philosophy, Shea, William R. and
      John King-Farlowe, eds. (New York: Science
      History Publications, 1976), pp. 49-65

1292. Clark, Lorenne. "Women and Locke: Who Owns the
      Apples in the Garden of Eden?" The Sexism of
      Social and Political Theory: Women and
      Reproduction from Plato to Nietzsche, Clarke,
      Lorenne and Lynda Lange, eds. (Toronto:
      University of Toronto Press, 1979).

1293. Clark, Loreene and Lynda Lange, eds. The Sexism
      of Social and Political Theory: Women and
      Reproduction from Plato to Nietzsche (Toronto:
      University of Toronto Press, 19790

1294. Clavir, Judith. "Choosing Either/Or: A Critique
      of Metaphysical Feminism," Feminist Studies,
      Vol. 5 (Summer 1979), pp. 402-410

1295. Collins, Margery and Christine Pierce. "Holes and Slime: Sexism in Sartre's Psychoanalysis," Women and Philosophy, Gould, Carol and Mary Wartofsky, eds. (New York: G. P. Putnam's Sons, 1976), pp. 112-127

1296. Cooke, Joanne; Charlotte Bunch-Weeks; and Robin Morgan, eds. The New Woman (Greenwich, CT: Fawcett, 1969)

1297. Cooper, James L. and Sheila McIsaac Cooper, eds. The Roots of American Feminist Thought (Boston: Allyn and Bacon, 1973)

1298. Coulson, Margaret et al. "The Housewife and Her Labor Under Capitalism—A Critique," New Left Review, No. 89 (Jan-Feb 1975), pp. 59-71

1299. Daly, Mary. Gyn/Ecology: The Metaethics of Radical Feminism (Boston: Beacon Press, 1978)

1300. Daly, Mary. Beyond God the Father (Boston: Beacon Press, 1973)

1301. Decter, Midge. The New Chastity and Other Arguments Against Women's Liberation (New York: Berkley Medallion Books, 1972)

1302. Deming, Barbara. Remembering Who We Are (Tallahassee, FL: Pagoda Publications, 1981)

1303. Deming, Barbara. We Cannot Live Without Our Lives (New York: Grossman Publishers, 1974)

1304. Devaki, Jain. "Can Feminism Be A Global Ideology?" Quest, Vol. 4 (Winter 1978), pp. 5-9

1305. Dickason, Anne. "Anatomy and Destiny: The Role of Biology in Plato's Views of Women," Women and Philosophy, Gould, Carol and Mary Wartofsky, eds. (New York: G. P. Putnam's Sons, 1976), pp. 112-127

1306. Dinnerstein, Dorothy. The Mermaid and the
      Minataur: Sexual Arrangements and the Human
      Malaise (New York: Harper Colophon, 1976)

1307. Dworkin, Andrea. Our Blood: Prophecies and
      Discourses on Sexual Politics (New York: Harper
      and Row, 1976)

1308. Dworkin, Andrea. Woman Hating: A Radical Look
      at Sexuality (New York: Dutton, 1974)

1309. Dworkin, R. J. "Ideology Formation: A Linear
      Structural Model of the Influences on Feminist
      Ideology," Sociological Quarterly, Vol. 20
      (Summer 1979), pp. 345-358

1310. Eisenstein, Hester and Alice Jardine, eds. The
      Future of Difference (Boston: G. K. Hall, 1980)

1311. Eisenstein, Zillah R., ed. Capitalist
      Patriarchy and the Case for Socialist Feminism
      (New York: Monthly Review, 1979)

1312. Eisenstein, Zillah R. The Radical Future of
      Liberal Feminism (New York: Longman, 1981)

1313. Elshtain, Jean Bethke, ed. The Family in
      Political Thought (Amherst, MA: University of
      Massachusetts Press, 1982).

1314. Elshtain, Jean Bethke. Public Man, Private
      Woman: Women in Social and Political Thought
      (Princeton, NJ: Princeton University Press,
      1981).

1315. Elshtain, Jean Bethke. "Against Androgyny,"
      Telos, Vol. 47 (Spring 1981), pp. 5-21

1316. Elshtain, Jean Bethke. "Doris Lessing:
      Language and Politics," Salmagundi, nos. 47-48
      (Winter-Spring 1980), pp. 95-114

1317. Elshtain, Jean Bethke. "Family Reconstruction," Commonweal, (August 1, 1980), pp. 430-431

1318. Elshtain, Jean Bethke. "Liberal Heresies: Existentialism and Repressive Feminism," Liberalism and the Modern Polity, McGrath, Michael C. Gargas, ed. (New York: Marcel Dekker, 1978), pp. 33-61

1319. Elshtain, Jean Bethke. "The Feminist Movement and the Question of Equality," Polity, Vol. 7 (1975), pp. 452-78

1320. Elshtain, Jean Bethke. "Moral Woman and Immoral Man: A Consideration of the Public-Private Split and Its Political Ramifications," Politics and Society, Vol. 4, No. 4, (1974), pp. 453-73

1321. Elshtain, Jean Bethke. "The Anti-Feminist Backlash," Commonweal, Vol. 8 (8 March 1974), pp. 16-19

1322. Engel, Stephanie. "Femininity as Tragedy: Re-Examining the New Narcissism," Socialist Review, Vol. 10 (September-October 1980), pp. 77-104

1323. Engels, Frederick. Origins of the Family, Private Property and the State (New York: Pathfinder Press, 1972)

1324. English, Jane, ed. Sex Equality (Englewood Cliffs, NJ: Prentice-Hall, 1977)

1325. Evans, Judith. "Women and Politics: A Re-Appraisal," Political Studies, Vol. 28 (June 1980), pp. 210-221.

1326. Farnsworth, Beatrice. "Bolshevism, the Woman Question and Alexandra Kollantai," American Historical Review, Vol. 81 (April 1976), pp. 292-316

1327. Ferguson, Ann. "Women as a New Revolutionary
      Class," Between Labor and Capital, Walker, Pat,
      ed. (Boston: South End Press, 1976),
      pp. 279-309

1328. Ferguson, Kathy E. Self, Society, and
      Womankind: The Dialectic of Liberation
      (Westport, CT: Greenwood Press, 1980)

1329. Ferguson, Kathy E. "Liberalism and Oppression:
      Emma Goldman and the Anarchist Feminist
      Alternative," Liberalism and the Modern Polity,
      McGrath, Michael C. Gangas, ed. (New York:
      Marcel Dekker, 1978), pp. 93-118

1330. Figes, Eva. Patriarchal Attitudes: Women in
      Society (London: Faber, 1970)

1331. Firestone, Shulamith. The Dialectic of Sex (New
      York: Bantam Books, 1976)

1332. Fisher, B. "Models Among Us: Social Authority
      and Political Activism," Feminist Studies, Vol.
      7 (Spring 1981), pp. 100-112.

1333. Fisher, Marguerite. "Eighteenth Century
      Theorists of Women's Liberation," Remember the
      Ladies: New Perspectives on Women in American
      History, George, Carol V. R., ed. (Syracuse,
      N.Y.: Syracuse University Press, 1975), pp.
      39-48

1334. Fishman, Walda Katz. The New Right:
      Unravelling the Opposition to Women's Equality
      (New York: Praeger Publishers, 1982)

1335. Flax, Jane. "Do Feminists Need Marxism?" Quest,
      Vol. 3 (Summer 1976), pp. 46-58

1336. Fluehr-Lobban, C. "Marxist Reappraisal of the
      Matriarchate," Current Anthropology, Vol. 20
      (June 1979), pp. 409-410; Discussion, Vol. 20,

pp. 608-611, pp. 814-820; Vol. 21 (June 1980),
pp. 409-410

1337. Foreman, Ann. Femininity as Alienation: Women
and the Family in Marxism and Psychoanalysis
(London: Pluto Press, 1977)

1338. Friedan, Betty. The Feminine Mystique (New
York: W. W. Norton, 1963)

1339. Friedan, Betty. It Changed My Life: Writings
on the Women's Movement (New York: Random
House, 1976)

1340. Friedan, Betty. The Second Stage (New York:
Summit Books, 1981)

1341. Freud, Sigmund. Civilization and Its
Discontents, Strachey, James, ed. and trans.,
(New York: W.W. Norton, 1962)

1342. Freud, Sigmund. "Lecture on Femininity," "Moses
and Monotheism," "Totem and Taboo," "The Case of
Dora," Introductory Lectures on Psychoanalysis,
Strachey, James, ed. and trans. (New York: W.W.
Norton, 1977)

1343. Fulenwider, Claire Knoche. Feminism in American
Politics: A Study of Ideological Influence (New
York: Praeger Publishers, 1980)

1344. Gardiner, Jean. "Women's Domestic Labor," New
Left Review, No. 89 (January 1975), pp. 47-58

1345. Garrison, Dee. "Karen Horney and Feminism,"
Signs, Vol. 6 (Summer 1981), pp. 672-691

1346. Gilman, Charlotte Perkins. Herland: A Lost
Feminist Utopian Novel (New York: Pantheon
Books, 1979)

1347. Glennon, Lynda M. Women and Dualism: A
      Sociology of Knowledge Analysis (New York:
      Longman and Co., 1979)

1348. Goldman, Alan H. Justice and Reverse
      Discrimination (Princeton, NJ: Princeton
      University Press, 1979)

1349. Goldstein, L. "Mill, Marx, and Women's
      Liberation," Journal of History and Philosophy,
      Vol. 18 (July 1980), pp. 319-334

1350. Gould, Carol. "The Woman Question: Philosophy
      of Liberation and the Liberation of Philosophy,"
      Women and Philosophy, Gould, Carol and Mary
      Wartofsky, eds. (New York: G. P. Putnam's
      Sons, 1976), pp. 5-44

1351. Gould, Carol and Mary Wartofsky, eds. Women and
      Philosophy (New York: G. P. Putnam's Sons,
      1976)

1352. Gould, John P. "Law, Custom and Myth: Aspects
      of the Social Position of Women in Classical
      Athens," The Journal of Hellenic Studies, Vol.
      100 (1980), pp. 38-59

1353. Griffin, Susan. Woman and Nature: The Roaring
      Inside Her (New York: Harper and Row, 1978)

1354. Grimes, Alan Pendleton. The Puritan Ethic and
      Woman Suffrage (Westport, CT: Greenwood Press,
      1980) reprint of 1967 edition

1355. Guettel, Charnie. Marxism and Feminism
      (Toronto: Women's Press, 1974)

1356. Gutmann, Amy. "Freud versus Feminism," Dissent,
      Vol. 26 (Spring 1979), pp. 204-12

1357. Hall, Nor. The Moon and the Virgin:
      Reflections on the Archetypal Feminine (New
      York: Harper & Row, 1980)

1358. Hamilton, Roberta. The Liberation of Women: A
      Study of Patriarchy and Capitalism (Winchester,
      MA: Allen & Unwin, 1978)

1359. Harding, Sandra. "The Social Function of the
      Empiricist Conception of Mind," Metaphilosophy,
      Vol. 10 (January 1979), pp. 38-47

1360. Hartmann, Heidi. "The Unhappy Marriage of
      Marxism and Feminism: Toward a More Progressive
      Union," Women and Revolution, Sargent, Lydia,
      ed. (Boston: South End Press, 1981), pp. 1-41

1361. Hartsock, Nancy. Money, Sex, and Power: An
      Essay on Domination and Community (New York:
      Longman, 1981)

1362. Hartsock, Nancy. "Feminist Theory and the
      Development of Revolutionary Strategy,"
      Capitalist Patriarchy and the Case for Socialist
      Feminism, Eisenstein, Zillah, ed. (New York:
      Monthly Review Press, 1979, pp. 56-82

1363. Hartsock, Nancy. "Political Change: Two
      Perspectives on Power," Quest, Vol. 1 (1974),
      pp. 10-25

1364. Heilbrun, Carolyn. Reinventing Womanhood (New
      York: W. W. Norton and Co., 1982)

1365. Heinen, Jacqueline. "Kollantai and the History
      of Women's Oppression," New Left Review, No. 110
      (July-August 1978), pp. 43-64

1366. Held, Virginia. "Marx, Sex, and the
      Transformation of Society," Women and
      Philosophy, Gould, Carol and Mary Wartofsky,
      eds. (New York: G. P. Putnam's Sons, 1976),
      pp. 168-184

1367. Hughes, P. "Reality Versus the Ideal: J. S.
      Mill's Treatment of Women, Workers and Private
      Property" (with reply by G. Feaver), Canadian

Journal of Political Science, Vol. 12 (Summer
1979), pp. 532-554; Discussion, Vol. 13
(December 1980), pp. 775-783

1368. Hume, David. A Treatise of Human Nature,
Selby-Bigge, L. A. and P. H. Nidditch, eds.
(Oxford: Oxford University Press, 1978)

1369. Hume, David. An Enquiry Concerning the
Principles of Morals included in Enquiries
Concerning the Human Understanding, 2nd ed.
Selby-Bigge, L. A., ed. (Westport, CT:
Greenwood Press, 1980), reprint of 1902 edition

1370. Janes, R. M. "On the Reception of Mary
Wollstonecraft's A Vindication of the Rights of
Women," Journal of the History of Ideas, Vol. 39
(April 1978), pp. 293-302

1371. Jenness, Linda, ed. Feminism and Socialism (New
York: Pathfinder Press, 1972)

1372. Keohane, Nannerl O. Philosophy and the State in
France: The Renaissance to the Enlightenment
(Princeton, NJ: Princeton University Press,
1980)

1373. Keohane, Nannerl O., Michelle Z. Rosaldo and
Barbara C. Gelpi, eds. Feminist Theory: A
Critique of Ideology (Chicago: University of
Chicago Press, 1982)

1374. Ketchum, Sara A. "Female Culture, Womanculture
and Conceptual Change: Toward a Philosophy of
Women's Studies," Social Theory and Practice,
Vol. 6 (Summer 1980), pp. 151-162

1375. Kollantai, Alexandra. "Social Basis of the
Woman Question" and "Morality and the New
Society," Selected Writings, Kollantai,
Alexandra, translation, introduction and
commentary by Alix Holt (New York: Norton,
1977).

1376. Kuhn, Annette and Annmarie Wolpe, eds. Feminism
      and Materialism: Women and Modes of Production
      (London: Routledge and Kegan Paul, 1978)

1377. Lange, Lynda. "Rousseau: Women and the General
      Will," The Sexism of Social and Political
      Theory: Women and Reproduction from Plato to
      Neitzsche, Clark, Lorenne and Lynda Lange, eds.
      (Toronto: University of Toronto Press, 1979),
      pp. 41-52

1378. Lenin, V. I. The Emancipation of Women: From
      the Writings of V.I. Lenin (New York:
      International Publishers, 1966)

1379. Locke, John. Two Treatises on Government,
      Laslett, Peter, ed. (New York: New American
      Library, 1965)

1380. Mahowald, Mary Briody, ed. Philosophy of Women:
      Classical to Current Concepts (Indianapolis, IN:
      Hackett Publishing, 1978)

1381. Marcil-Lacoste, Louise. "The Consistency of
      Hume's Position Concerning Women," Dialogue,
      Vol. 15 (September 1976), pp. 425-40

1382. Marcuse, Herbert. "Marxism and Feminism,"
      Women's Studies, Vol. 2, No. 3 (1974), pp.
      279-288

1383. Marks, Elaine and Isabelle de Courtivran, eds.
      New French Feminisms (Amherst, MA: University
      of Massachusetts Press, 1979)

1384. Marx, Karl. On Education, Women and Children,
      Padover, Saul, ed. and trans. in the Karl Marx
      Library, Vol. 6 (New York: McGraw-Hill, 1975)

1385. McCormack, Thelma. "Good Theory or Just Theory?
      Toward a Feminist Philosophy of Social Science,"
      Women's Studies International Quarterly, Vol. 4,
      No. 1 (1981), pp. 1-12

1386. McGrath, Michael C. Gargas, ed. Liberalism and
      the Modern Polity (New York: Marcel Dekker,
      1978)

1387. Meilaender, Gilbert. "'A Little Monarchy':
      Hobbes on the Family," Thought, Vol. 53
      (December 1978), pp. 40-415

1388. Meulenbelt, Anja. "On the Political Economy of
      Domestic Labor" trans. from the Dutch in Quest,
      Vol. 4 (Winter 1978), pp. 18-31

1389. Mill, John Stuart. On Liberty (Chicago: Henry
      Regnery, 1956)

1390. Mill, John Stuart. On the Subjection of Women
      (Greenwich, CT: Fawcett, 1970)

1391. Mill, John Stuart and Harriet Taylor. Essays on
      Sex Equality, Rossi, Alice, ed. (Chicago:
      University of Chicago Press, 1970)

1392. Miller, Sally M., ed. Flawed Liberation:
      Socialism and Feminism (Westport, CT:
      Greenwood Press, 1981)

1393. Millett, Kate. Sexual Politics (Garden City,
      NY: Doubleday, 1970)

1394. Mitchell, Juliet. Psychoanalysis and Feminism:
      Freud, Reich, Laing and Women (New York:
      Random House, 1975)

1395. Mitchell, Juliet. Women's Estate (New York:
      Vintage Books, 1973)

1396. Mitchell, Juliet. "Marxism and Women's
      Liberation," Social Praxis, Vol. 1 (1973), pp.
      11-22

1397. Molloy, Alice. In Other Words (Toronto:
      Women's Press Collective, 1977)

1398. Mora, F. "Metaphysical Purdah," Philosophy,
      Vol. 55 (July 1980), pp. 377-385

1399. Moraga, Cherrie and Gloria Anzaldua, eds. This
      Bridge called My Back: Writings by Radical
      Women of Color (Watertown, MA: Persephone
      Press, 1981)

1400. Morgan, Marabel. The Total Woman (Old Tappan,
      NJ: Fleming H. Revell Co., 1973)

1401. Morgan, Robin, ed. Sisterhood Is Powerful: An
      Anthology of Writings from the Women's
      Liberation Movement (New York: Random House,
      1970)

1402. Moulton, Janice. "The Myth of the Neutral Man,"
      Feminism and Philosophy, Vetterling-Braggin,
      Mary; Frederick Elliston; and Jane English, eds.
      (Totowa, NJ: Rowan and Littlefield, 1977), pp.
      124-137

1403. O'Brien, Mary. "Reproducing Marxist Man," The
      Sexism of Social and Political Theory: Women
      and Reproduction from Plato to Nietzsche, Clark,
      Lorenne and Lynda Lange, eds. (Toronto:
      University of Toronto Press, 1979), pp. 99-116

1404. O'Brien, Mary. "The Politics of Impotence,"
      Contemporary Issues in Political Philosophy,
      Shea, William R. and John King-Farlowe, eds.
      (New York: Science History Publications, 1976),
      pp. 147-162

1405. O'Hare, Kate Richards. Selected Writings and
      Speeches, Foner, Philip S. and Sally M. Miller,
      eds. (Baton Rouge, LA: Louisiana State
      University Press, 1982)

1406. Okin, Susan Moller. Women in Western Political
      Thought (Princeton, N.J.: Princeton University
      Press, 1979)

1407. Okin, Susan Moller. "Philosopher Queens and Private Wives--Plato on Women and the Family," Philosophy and Public Affairs, Vol. 6 (Summer 1977), pp. 345-369

1408. Osborne, Martha Lee. "Plato's Unchanging View of Women: A Denial that Anatomy Spells Destiny," The Philosophical Forum, Vol. 6 (Summer 1975), pp. 447-452

1409. Pateman, Carole. "Disorder of Women: Women, Love, and the Sense of Justice," Ethics, Vol. 91 (October 1980), pp. 20-34

1410. Pateman, Carole. "Women, Nature, and the Suffrage (review article)," Ethics, Vol. 90, (July 1980), pp. 564-575

1411. Pateman, Carole. "Women and Consent," Political Theory, Vol. 8 (May 1980), pp. 149-168

1412. Pennock, J. H. and R. Chapman. Equality (Nomos IX), (New York: Atherton, 1967)

1413. Pierce, Christine. "Review Essay: Philosophy," Signs, Vol. 1 (Winter 1975), pp. 487-503

1414. Pierce, Christine. "Equality: Republic V," The Monist, Vol. 57 (January 1973), pp. 1-11

1415. Piercy, Marge. Woman on the Edge of Time (New York: Fawcett, 1978)

1416. Piercy, Marge. Living in the Open (New York: Alfred Knopf, 1976)

1417. Piercy, Marge. To Be of Use (New York: Doubleday & Co., 1973)

1418. Pomeroy, Sarah B. Goddesses, Whores, Wives and Slaves: Women in Classical Antiquity (New York: Schocken Books, 1976)

1419. Pomeroy, Sarah B. "Selected Bibliography on Women in Antiquity," Arethusa, Vol. 6 (Spring 1973), pp. 125-127

1420. The Quest staff. Building Feminist Theory (New York: Longman, 1981)

1421. Rapaport, Elizabeth. "On the Future of Love: Rousseau and the Radical Feminists," Women and Philosophy: Toward a Theory of Liberation, Gould, Carol and Mary Wartofsky, eds. (New York: G. P. Putnam's Son, 1976), pp. 185-205

1422. Rawls, John. A Theory of Justice (Cambridge, MA: Harvard University, 1975)

1423. Reed, Evelyn. Problems of Women's Liberation: A Marxist Approach (New York: Merit Publishers, 1972)

1424. Reiter, Rayna R., ed. Toward an Anthropology of Women (New York: Monthly Review Press, 1975)

1425. Reuther, Rosemary. "Why Socialism Needs Feminism and Vice Versa," Christianity and Crisis, Vol. 40 (April 28, 1980), pp. 103-108

1426. Rich, Adrienne. On Lies, Secrets and Silence (New York: W. W. Norton & Co., Inc., 1979)

1427. Rosaldo, Michelle and Louise Lamphere, eds. Woman, Culture and Society (Stanford, CA: Stanford University Press, 1974)

1428. Rosenberg, Rosalind. Beyond Separate Spheres: Intellectual Roots of Modern Feminism (New Haven, CT: Yale University Press, 1982)

1429. Rosenfelt, Deborah S. Strong Women (Old Westbury, NY: Feminist Press, 1976)

1430. Rossi, Alice, ed. The Feminist Papers: From
      Adams to de Beauvoir (New York: Columbia
      University, 1973)

1431. Rousseau, Jean-Jacques. Emile, (London: Dent,
      1969)

1432. Rousseau, Jean-Jacques. La Nouvelle Heloise:
      Julie or, the New Eloise, McDowell, Judith H.,
      trans. and abridg. (University Park, PA:
      Pennsylvania State University, 1968)

1433. Rover, Constance. Love, Morals and the
      Feminists (Boston: Routledge and Kegan Paul,
      1970)

1434. Rowbotham, Sheila. Woman's Consciousness, Man's
      World (Baltimore, MD: Penguin Books, 1973)

1435. Rowbotham, Sheila. Women, Resistance and
      Revolution (New York: Vintage Books, 1972)

1436. Rubin, Gayle. "The Traffic in Women: Notes on
      the 'Political Economy of Sex,'" Toward An
      Anthropology of Women, Reiter, Rayna, ed. (New
      York: Monthly Review Press, 1975)

1437. Ruther, Rosemary, ed. Religion and Sexism:
      Images of Women in the Jewish and Christian
      Traditions (New York: Simon and Schuster, 1974)

1438. Sabrosky, Judith A. From Rationality to
      Liberation: The Evolution of Feminist Ideology
      (Westport, CT: Greenwood Press, 1979)

1439. Sacks, Karen. Sisters and Wives: The Past and
      Future of Sexual Equality (Westport, CT:
      Greenwood Press, 1979)

1440. Saffioti, Heleieth. Women in Class Society
      (New York: Monthly Review Press, 1978)

1441. Sargent, Lydia, ed. Woman and Revolution: A
Discussion of the Unhappy Marriage of Marxism
and Feminism (Boston: South End Press, 1981)

1442. Saxonhouse, Arlene. "Men, Women, War and
Politics: 'Family and Polis' in Aristophanes
and Euripides," Political Theory, Vol. 8
(February 1980), pp. 65-81

1443. Saxonhouse, Arlene. "Philosopher and Female in
the Political Thought of Plato," Political
Theory, Vol. 4 (May 1976), pp. 195-212

1444. Schaar, John. "Equality of Opportunity and
Beyond," in his Legitimacy in the Modern State
(New Brunswick, NJ: Transaction Books, 1981)

1445. Schafly, Phyllis. The Power of Christian Woman
(Cincinnati, OH: Standard Publishing Co., 1981)

1446. Schafly, Phyllis. The Power of the Positive
Woman (Westport, CT: Arlington House, 1977)

1447. Schneir, Miriam, comp. Feminism: The Essential
Historical Writings (New York: Vintage Books,
1977)

1448. Schochet, Gordon. Patriarchialism and Political
Thought: The Authoritarian Family and Political
Speculation and Attitudes Especially in the 17th
Century (Oxford: Blackwell, 1975)

1449. Schochet, Gordon. "Thomas Hobbes on the Family
and the State of Nature," Political Science
Quarterly, Vol. 82 (September 1967), pp. 427-445

1450. Scott, Heide. Does Socialism Liberate Women?
(Boston: Beacon Press, 1974)

1451. Schramm, Sarah Slavin. Plow Women Rather Than
Reapers: An Intellectual History of Feminism in
the United States (Metuchen, NJ: Scarecrow
Press, 1979)

1452. Schwartz, Nancy L. "Distinction between Public and Private Life: Marx on the Zoon Politicon," Political Theory, Vol. 7 (May 1979), pp. 245-266

1453. Secombe, Wally. "The Housewife and Her Labor Under Capitalism," New Left Review, No. 83 (Jan-Feb 1974), pp. 3-24

1454. Shanley, Mary Lyndon. "Marriage Contract and Social Contract in Seventeenth Century English Political Thought," Western Political Quarterly, Vol. 32 (March 1979), pp. 79-91

1455. Shanley, Mary Lyndon. "Invisible Women: Thoughts on Teaching Political Philosophy," News (for Teachers of Political Science), (Winter 1979), p. 2

1456. Slater, Phillip. The Glory of Hera: Greek Mythology and The Greek Family (Boston, 1968)

1457. Smith, Dorothy E. Feminism and Marxism: A Place to Begin, A Way to Go (Vancouver, BC: New Star Books, 1977)

1458. Tatalovich, Anne. "John Stuart Mill's The Subjection of Women: An Analysis," Southern Quarterly, Vol. 12 (October 1973), pp. 87-105

1459. "Toward a Feminist Theory of Motherhood," Feminist Studies, Vol. 4 (June 1978), Special Issue

1460. Trotsky, L. Women and the Family (New York: Pathfinder Press, 1970)

1461. Vetterling-Braggin, Mary; Frederick Elliston; and Jane English. Feminism and Philosophy (Totowa, NJ: Rowan and Littlefield, 1977)

1462. Vogel, Lise. "The Earthly Family," Radical America, Vol. 7 (July-October 1973), pp. 9-50

1463. Weinbaum, Batya. The Curious Courtship of
      Women's Liberation and Socialism (Boston: South
      End Press, 1978)

1464. Wender, Dorothea. "Plato: Misogynist,
      Paedophite and Feminist," Arethusa, Vol. 6
      (Spring 1973), pp. 75-90

1465. Wexler, Victor G. "Made for Man's Delight:
      Rousseau as Antifeminist," American Historical
      Review, Vol. 81 (April 1976), pp. 266-291

1466. White, Stephen W. "Beautiful Losers: An
      Analysis of Radical Feminist Egalitarianism,"
      The Journal of Value Inquiry, Vol. 11 (Winter
      1977), pp. 264-283

1467. Williford, Miriam. "Bentham on the Rights of
      Women," Journal of the History of Ideas, Vol. 36
      (January 1975), pp. 167-176

1468. Wittig, Monique. Lesbian Body (New York: Avon
      Books, 1976)

1469. Wolgast, Elizabeth H. Equality and the Rights
      of Woman (Ithaca, NY: Cornell University Press,
      1980)

1470. Wollstonecraft, Mary. A Vindication of the
      Rights of Women, Hagelman, Charles W. Jr., ed.
      (New York: W. W. Norton, 1967)

1471. Wollstonecraft, Mary. Vindication of the Rights
      of Men, Introduction by Eleanor Louise Nichols;
      (Delmar, NY: Scholars' Facsimiles and
      Reprints, 1960), reprint of 1790 edition

1472. Wollstonecraft, Mary. Maria; or, the Wrongs of
      Women (New York: W. W. Norton, 1975), New
      Edition

1473. Wollstonecraft, Mary. <u>Mary, A Fiction</u>(...),
      Luria, Gina, ed. (New York: Garland
      Publishing, Inc., 1974), reprint of 1788
      edition.

1474. Young, Iris. "Socialist Feminism and the Limits
      of Dual Systems Theory," <u>Socialist Review</u>, Vol
      10 (March-June 1980), pp. 169-188

XIII. REFERENCE RESOURCES IN WOMEN AND POLITICS

1475. Adams, Edith L. Where to Find Foundation Money
for Women's Projects: A Directory to Who's
Giving Money to Women's Projects (Yonkers, NY:
Independent Women's Press, 1977)

1476. Albatross, P.O. Box 2016, Central Station, East
Organe, NJ, 07019. Poetry. Vol. 1 (San
Francisco, CA: The Bindweed Press, 1963)
December

1477. Aldous, Joan and Reuben Hill. International
Bibliography of Research in Marriage and Family,
1900-1964 (Minneapolis, MN: Distributed by the
University of Minnesota Press for the Minnesota
Family Study Center and the Institute of Life
Insurance, 1967)

1478. Allen, Martha Leslie, ed. Index/Directory of
Women's Media, (Washington, DC: Women's
Institute for Freedom of the Press, 1981)

1479. The American Jewish Woman, 1654-1980: A
Documentary History (New York: KTAV Publishing
House, 1981) Published jointly with the
American Jewish Archives, Cincinnati, Ohio.
Completes a supplement to The American Jewish
Woman, 1654-1980

1480. Arthur and Elizabeth Schlesinger Library on the
History of Women in America. The Manuscript

177

Inventories and the Catalogs of Manuscripts,
Books, and Pictures, Radcliffe College,
Cambridge, Massachusetts (Boston: G. K. Hall,
1973)

1481. Astin, Helen S.; Nancy Suniewick; and Susan
Dweck. Women: A Bibliography of Their
Education and Careers (Washington, DC: Human
Service Press, 1971)

1482. Ausman, Jon M. Published Works on Women and
Politics (Monticello, IL: Vance Bibliographies,
April 1979)

1483. Ballou, Patricia. Women: A Bibliography of
Bibliographies (Boston: G. K. Hall and Co.,
1980)

1484. Bannon, Robert. "Dual Earner Families: An
Annotated Bibliography," Monthly Labor Review,
Vol. 104 (February 1981), pp. 53-59

1485. Barrer, Myra E., ed. Women's Organizations and
Leaders (Washington, DC: Today Publications
and News Service, 1973, updated 1975-76)

1486. Baxandall, Rosalyn; Linda Gordon; and Susan
Reverby, eds. America's Working Women: A
Documentary History--1600 to the Present (New
York: A Vintage Book, 1982)

1487. Blumhagen, Katherine O'Conner and Walter D.
Johnson. Women's Studies: An Interdisciplinary
Collection (Westport, CT: Greenwood Press,
1978)

1488. Boneparth, Ellen. "Integrating Materials on
Women," News (for Teachers of Political
Science), (Summer 1980), p. 1

1489. Brownlee, W. Elliot and Mary M. Brownlee. Women
in the American Economy: A Documentary History,

1675 to 1929 (New Haven, CT: Yale University
Press, 1976)

1490. Buvinic, Mayra. Women and World Development:
An Annotated Bibliography (Washington, DC:
Overseas Development Council, 1976)

1491. Cantor, Aviva. A Bibliography on the Jewish
Woman: A Comprehensive and Annotated Listing of
Works Published, 1900-1978 (Fresh Meadow, NY:
Biblio Press, 1979)

1492. The Center for the American Woman and Politics,
Eagleton Institute of Politics, Rutgers-The
State University of New Jersey. Women in Public
Office: A Bibliographical Directory and
Statistical Analysis (Metuchen, NJ: Scarecrow
Press, 1978, second edition)

1493. Ceulemans, Miek. Mass Media: The Image, Role,
and Social Conditions of Women: A Collection
and Analysis of Research Materials (New York:
United Nations Education, Scientific and
Cultural Organizations, 1979)

1494. Conditions, P. O. Box 56, Van Brunt Station,
Brooklyn, New York, 11215. Begins 1976. A
magazine of writing by women with an emphasis on
writing by Lesbians.

1495. Cummings, Bernice and Victoria Schuck. Women
Organizing: An Anthology (Metuchen, NJ:
Scarecrow Press, 1979)

1496. Diner, Hasia R. Women and Urban Society: A
Guide to Information Sources (Detroit, MI: Gale
Research Co., 1979)

1497. Edry, Carol F. and Ginnie Goulet, eds. Women's
Yellow Pages, 1974: The Original Sourcebook for
Women (Boston: Boston Women's Collective, Inc.,
1973)

1498. Een, JoAnn Delores and Marie B.
      Rosenberg-Dishman. Women and Society, Citations
      3601 to 6000: An Annotated Bibliography
      (Beverly Hills, CA: Sage Publications, 1978)
      [Intended as Vol. 2 of Rosenberg and Bergstrom,
      comps., Women and Society, see page 187]

1499. Eichler, Margrit. An Annotated Selected
      Bibliography of Bibliographies on Women (Ottawa:
      Association of Universities and Colleges of
      Canada, Committee on the Status of Women, 1973)

1500. Ellison, Charles E. Women and Citizen
      Participation: A Selected Bibliography
      (Monticello, IL: Vance Bibliographies, March
      1981)

1501. Equal Rights Amendment Project. The Equal
      Rights Amendment: A Bibliographic Study
      (Westport, CT: Greenwood Press, 1976)

1502. Faunce, Patricia Spencer. Women and Ambition:
      A Bibliography (Metuchen, NJ: Scarecrow Press,
      1980)

1503. Feminist Review. Begins in 1979. A journal
      seeking to formulate a new analysis to correct
      the inadequacies of established theories
      regarding women, published in London

1504. Feminist Studies. Begins summer 1972. A forum
      for feminist analysis, debate and exchange
      committed to changing women's conditions

1505. First Person Female American: A Selected and
      Annotated Bibliography of the Autobiographies of
      American Women Living After 1950, Briscoe, Mary
      Louise, ed. (Troy, NY: Whitston Publishing Co.,
      1980)

1506. Fishburn, Katherine. Women in Popular Culture:
      A Reference Guide (Westport, CT: Greenwood
      Press, 1982)

1507. Forerunner. Vols. 1-7 (all publ.) (Westport, CT: Greenwood Press, 1968) reprinted from 1909-1916, bound in 7 volumes

1508. Frey, Linda; Marsha Frey; and Joanne Schneider, eds. Women in Western European History: A Select Chronological, Geographical, and Topical Bibliography from Antiquity to the French Revolution (Westport, CT: Greenwood Press, 1982)

1509. Friedman, Leslie. Sex Roles Stereotyping in the Mass Media: An Annotated Bibliography (New York: Garland Publishing, Inc., 1977)

1510. Frontiers. Begins in 1975. A journal of women's studies to bridge the gap between university and community women

1511. Gager, Nancy, ed. Women's Rights Almanac (Bethesda, MD: Elizabeth Cady Stanton Publishing Co., 1974)

1512. Garrison, Carole G. "Simulating a Political Convention for a Women's Studies Course," News (for Teachers of Political Science), (Summer 1981), p. 1

1513. Goehlert, Robert. Political Attitudes: A Bibliography (Monticello, IL: Vance Bibliographies, October 1981)

1514. Gold, Doris B. Opposition to Voluntarism: An Annotated Bibliography (Monticello, IL: Council of Planning Librarians, June 1979)

1515. Green, Rayna. Native American Women: A Biblography (Washington, DC: U.S. Department of Education, 1981)

1516. Haber, Barbara. Women in America: A Guide to Books, 1963-1975 (Boston: G.K. Hall, 1978)

1517. Harrell, Karen Fair. Women in the Armed Forces:
A Bibliography, 1970-1980 (Monticello, IL:
Vance Bibliographies, June 1980)

1518. Harrison Cynthia. Women in American History: A
Bibliography (Santa Barbara, CA: ABC-Clio,
1979)

1519. Herstory. Microfilm Collection: Table of
Contents, 1971- (Wooster, OH: Issued by the
Women's History Library and the Micro Photo
Division of Bell and Howell, Co., 1971)

1520. Hindings, Andrea, ed. Women's History Sources:
A Guide to Archives and Manuscript Collections
in the United States (New York: R.R. Bowker,
Co., 1979)

1521. ten Houton, Elizabeth S. "Some Collections of
Special Use for Women's History Resources in the
United States," AAUW (American Association of
University Women) Journal, Vol. 67 (April 1974),
pp. 35-35

1522. Howes, Durwood, ed. American Women, 1935-1940:
A Composite Biographical Dictionary (Detroit,
MI: Gale Research Co., 1981)

1523. Hypatia. Forthcoming spring 1983. A journal
focused on women and philosophy

1524. Internationaal Archief voor de Vrouwenbeweging.
Catalogue of the Library of the International
Archives for the Women's Movement, Amsterdam
(Boston: G.K. Hall, 1980)

1525. Ireland, Norma Olin. Index to Women in the
World From Ancient to Modern Times: Biographies
and Portraits (Westwood, MA: F.W. Faxon Co.,
1970)

1526. Jacobs, Sue-Ellen. Women in Perspective; A Guide for Cross-Cultural Studies (Urbana, IL: University of Illinois Press, 1974)

1527. Kennedy, Susan Estabrook. America's White Working-class Women: A Historical Bibliography (New York: Garland Publishing, Inc., 1981)

1528. Kirkpatrick, Meredith. Women in the Public Service: A Selective Bibliography (Monticello, IL: Council of Planning Librarians, February 1978)

1529. Kleiman, Carol. Women's Networks: The Complete Guide to Getting a Better Job, Advancing Your Career, and Feeling Great as a Woman Through Networking (Philadelphia, PA: Lippincott and Crowell, Pubs., 1980)

1530. Klein, Susan and Veronica G. I. Thomas. Sex Equity in Education: NIE Sponsored Projects and Publications (U.S. Department of Education, National Institute of Education, National Institute of Education), (Washington, DC: U.S. Government Printing Office, 1981)

1531. Klotman, Phyllis R. and Wilmer H. Baatz. The Black Family and the Black Woman: A Bibliography (New York: Arno Press, 1978)

1532. Knaster, Meri. Women in Spanish America: An Annotated Bibliography from Conquest to Contemporary Times (Boston: G.K. Hall, 1977)

1533. Kohen, Andrew I. et al. Women and the Economy: A Bibliography and a Review of the Literature on Sex Differentiation in the Labor Market (Columbus, OH: Center for Human Resource Research, Ohio State University, March 1975)

1534. Kowalski, Rosemary Ribich. Women and Film: A Bibliography (Metuchen, NJ: Scarecrow Press, 1976)

1535. Krichmar, Albert, assisted by Virginia Carlson
Smith and Ann E. Wiederrecht. The Women's
Movement in the Seventies: An International
English-Language Bibliography (Metuchen, NJ:
Scarecrow Press, 1977)

1536. Krichmar, Albert, comp. Women's Studies: A
Guide to Publications and Services Available in
the Library of the University of Santa Barbara
and in the Santa Barbara Area (Santa Barbara,
CA: Librarian's Office, Library, University of
California, Santa Barbara, January 1975)

1537. Krichmar, Albert. The Women's Rights Movement
in the United States, 1848-1970: A Bibliography
and Sourcebook (Metuchen, NJ: Scarecrow Press,
1972)

1538. La Mujer Chicana: An Annotated Bibliography
(Austin, TX: Chicana Research and Learning
Center, 1976)

1539. Leavitt, Judith A. Women in Management,
1970-1979: A Bibliography (Monticello, IL:
Council of Planning Librarians, October 1980)

1540. Leonard, Eugenie and Drinker, Sophia. The
American Woman in Colonial and Revolutionary
Times: 1565-1800: A Syllabus with Bibliography
(Westport, CT: Greenwood Press, 1975), reprint
of 1962 edition

1541. Lerner, Gerda, ed. Black Women in White
America: A Documentary History (New York:
Vintage Books, 1982)

1542. Lesbian Herstory Archives. (Lesbian Herstory
Educational Foundation, Inc., P.O. Box 1258, New
York, NY 10001)

1543. Levenson, Rosaline. Women in Government and
Politics: A Bibliography of American and

Foreign Sources (Monticello, IL: Council of Planning Librarians, November 1973)

1544. Lynn, Naomi B.; Ann B. Matasar; and Marie Barovic Rosenberg. Research Guide in Women's Studies (Morristown, NJ: General Learning Press, 1974)

1545. McKee, Kathleen Burke. Women's Studies: A Guide to Reference Sources (Storrs, CT: University of Connecticut Library, 1977)

1546. McPhee, Carol and Ann FitzGerald, comps. Feminist Quotations: Voices of Rebels, Reformers and Visionaries (New York: Crowell, 1979)

1547. Manning, Beverley. Index to American Women Speakers, 1828-1978 (Metuchen, NJ: Scarecrow Press, 1980)

1548. Mehlman, Terry. The Annotated Guide to Women's Periodicals in the United States (Richmond, IN: Terry Mehlman, 1982)

1549. National Directory of Women Elected Officials, 1981 (New York: Jeanine Dowling, Philip Morris, Inc., 1981) (Published by the National Women's Political Caucus)

1550. Newman, Joan E. Girls Are People Too!: A Bibliography of Nontraditional Female Roles in Children's Books (Metuchen, NJ: Scarecrow Press, 1982)

1551. Notable American Women: 1607-1950: A Biographical Dictionary, 3 Vols., James, Edward T. and Janet W. James, eds. (Cambridge, MA: Harvard University Press, 1971)

1552. Notable American Women: The Modern Period, A Bibliographical Dictionary, Sicherman, Barbara,

et al., eds. (Cambridge, MA: Harvard University
Press, 1980)

1553. Oakes, Elizabeth H. Guide to Social Science
Resources in Women's Studies (Santa Barbara, CA:
ABC-Clio Books, 1978)

1554. Off Our Backs, 1724 20th Street, NW, Washington,
DC, 20009. Begins 1970, 11 per year. One of
the earliest feminist tabloids covering a full
range of feminist interests.

1555. Papachristou, Judith. Women Together: A
History in Documents of the Women's Movement in
the United States (New York: Knopf Books, 1976)

1556. Paramore, Katherine. Nontraditional Job
Training for Women: A Bibliography and Resource
Directory for Employment and Training Planners
(Monticello, IL: Council of Planning
Librarians, February 1981)

1557. Parker, Franklin and Betty June Parker, eds.
Women's Education, A World View: Annotated
Bibliography of Doctoral Dissertations
(Westport, CT: Greenwood Press, 1979)

1558. Parker, William. Homosexuality: A Selective
Bibliography of over 3,000 Items (Metuchen, NJ:
Scarecrow Press, 1971)

1559. Pethick, Jane, comp. Battered Wives: A Select
Bibliography (Toronto: Center of Criminology,
University of Toronto, January 1979)

1560. Pomeroy, Sarah B. "Selected Bibliography on
Women in Antiquity," Arethusa, Vol. 6 (Spring
1973) pp. 125-127

1561. Quest: A Feminist Quarterly. Begins in 1974. A
journal dedicated to working toward achieving

the radical change in society required to
transform the lives of women.

1562. Remley, Mary L. <u>Women in Sport: A Guide to
Information Sources</u> (Detroit, MI: Gale Research
Co., 1980)

1563. Rennie, Susan and Kirsten Grimstad, eds. <u>The
New Woman's Survival Sourcebook</u> (New York:
Knopf Books, 1975)

1564. Ritchie, Maureen. <u>Women's Studies: A Checklist
of Bibliographies</u> (London: Mansell, 1980)

1565. Roberts, J. R. <u>Black Lesbians: An Annotated
Bibliography</u> (Tallahassee, FL: Naiad Press,
Inc., 1981)

1566. Rosenberg, Marie Barovic and Len V. Bergstrom,
comps. and eds. <u>Women and Society: A Critical
Review of the Literature With a Selected
Annotated Bibliography</u> (Beverly Hills, CA: Sage
Publications, 1975) [for Vol. 2 see Een and
Rosenburg-Dishman, p. 180]

1567. Rushing, A. B. "Annotated Bibliography of Black
Women in Black Literature," <u>CLA Journal</u>, Vol. 21
(March 1978), pp. 435-442

1568. <u>Sage Family Study Abstracts</u>, Vol. 1, February
1979- (Beverly Hills, CA: Sage Publications,
1979)

1569. <u>Salaries and Women in White-Collar Work. A
Selective Bibliography, 1954-1979</u> (Monticello,
IL: Vance Bibliographies, May 1981)

1570. Schlachter, Gail and A. Belli-Donn. <u>Minorities
and Women: A Guide to Reference Literature in
the Social Sciences</u> (Los Angeles, CA: Reference
Service Press, 1977)

1571. Signs. Begins autumn 1975, a journal of women in culture and society. Described by Katz and Katz in Magaziness for Libraries as the most scholarly women's studies journal in the United States

1572. Sims, Janet L., ed. The Progress of Afro-- American Women: A Selected Bibliography and Resource Guide (Westport, CT: Greenwood Press, 1980

1573. Sims, Janet L. Black Women in the Employment Sector (Monticello, IL: Vance Bibliographies, May 1979)

1574. Sinister Wisdom. Michelle Cliff and Adrienne Rich, P.O. Box 66, Amherst, MA 01004. Begins 1976, quarterly. A journal of words and pictures for the lesbian imagination in all women

1575. Soltow, Martha Jane and Mary K. Wery. American Women and the Labor Movement, 1825-1974: An Annotated Bibliography (Metuchen, NJ: Scarecrow Press, 1976)

1576. Sophia Smith Collection. Catalogs of the Sophia Smith Collection, Women's History Archive, Smith College, Northampton, Massachusetts (Boston: G.K. Hall, 1975)

1577. "Sources for the 'New Women's History,'" American Archivist, Vol. 43 (Spring 1980), pp. 180-190

1578. Stanwick, Kathy and Christine Li. The Political Participation of Women in the United States: A Selected Bibliography, 1950-1976 (Metuchen, NJ: Scarecrow Press, 1977) (Prepared under the auspices of The Center for The American Woman and Politics, Eagleton Institute, Rutgers - The State University of New Jersey)

1579. Stern, Jean. A List of Library Holdings of Feminist Periodicals, Newspapers and Microforms as of July 1978 (San Diego, CA: San Diego State University Library, 1978)

1580. Stineman, Esther. American Political Women: Contemporary and Historical Profiles (Littleton, CO: Libraries Unlimited, 1980)

1581. Stineman, Esther. Womens' Studies: A Recommended Core Bibliography (Littleton, CO: Libraries Unlimited, 1979)

1582. Sullivan, Kaye. Films For, By and About Women (Metuchen, NJ: Scarecrow Press, 1980)

1583. Swanick, Margaret Lynne Struthers. Women and Pensions: A Checklist of Publications (Monticello, IL: Vance Bibliographies, July 1979)

1584. Swanick, Margaret Lynne Struthers. Women as Administrators: A Selected Bibliography (Monticello, IL: Vance Bibliographies, October 1978)

1585. Swanson, Kathryn. Affirmative Action and Preferential Admissions in Higher Education: An Annotated Bibliography (Metuchen, NJ: Scarecrow Press, Inc., 1981)

1586. Terris, Virginia R. Woman in America: A Guide to Information Sources (Detroit, MI: Gale Research Co., 1980)

1587. Tiffany, S. W. "Anthropology and the Study of Women; Review Article," American Anthropologists, Vol. 82 (June 1980), pp. 374-380

1588. Tilly, Louise A. "Social Sciences and the Study of Women," Comparative Study of Society and History, Vol. 20 (January 1978), pp. 163-173

1589. Tingley, Elizabeth and Donald F. Tingley. Women and Feminism in American History: A Guide to Information Services (Detroit, MI: Gale Research Co., 1981)

1590. Turner, Maryann. Biblioteca Femina: A Herstory of Book Collections Concerning Women (Warrensburg, NY: Buckwheat Turner, 1978)

1591. United States Bureau of the Census, Population Division. A Statistical Portrait of Women in the United States: 1978 (Current Population Reports) (Washington, DC: U. S. Government Printing Office, February 1980)

1592. United States Office of Education, Women's Educational Equity Communications Network. Resources in Women's Educational Equity (Washington, DC: U.S. Government Printing Office, November 1978)

1593. Vaughan, Nigel; Robert Slater; and Charles Jackson. The Psychological and Social Implications of the Entrance of Women into the Labor Force: An Annotated Bibliography of Source Material (Monticello, IL: Council of Planning Librarians, December 1980)

1594. Washington (State). State Library. Women; Their Struggle for Equality: A Selected Bibliography (Washington, DC: State Library, September 1977, second edition)

1595. Weis, Ina J. Women in Politics: A Bibliography (Monticello, IL: Vance Bibliographies, 1979)

1596. Wheeler, Helen Rippier. Womanhood Media: Current Resources About Women (Metuchen, NJ: Scarecrow Press, 1972)

1597. Wheeler, Helen Rippier. Womanhood Media
Supplement: Additional Current Resources about
Women (Metuchen, NJ: Scarecrow Press, 1975)

1598. Who's Who of American Women, Marquis, George
Prior, ed. (Chicago, IL: Marquis Who's Who,
Inc., biennially from 1958)

1599. Wilcox, Laird M., comp. Directory of the
American Left, 1980: A Current and
Comprehensive Directory and Guide to Socialist,
Communist, Collectivist, Environmentalist,
Feminist, Disarmament, Welfare Statistics,
Liberal and Other Left Wing Organisations and
Periodicals in the United States, Canada and the
British Commonwealth (Kansas City, MO:
Editorial Research Service, 1979)

1600. Wilkins, Kay S. Women's Education in the United
States: A Guide to Information Sources
(Detroit, MI: Gale Research Co., 1979)

1601. Williams, Ora. American Black Women in the Arts
and Social Sciences: A Bibliographic Survey;
Revised and Expanded Edition (Metuchen, NJ:
Scarecrow Press, 1978)

1602. Williamson, Jane. New Feminist Scholarship: A
Guide to Bibliographies (Old Westury, NY:
Feminist Press, 1979)

1603. Women in Politics. Begins Spring 1979. A
multi-disciplinary journal exploring women in
politics with a variety of methods.

1604. Women in Public Office: A Biographical
Directory and Statistical Analysis (Metuchen,
NJ: Scarecrow Press, 1978)

1605. Women Studies Abstracts, (Rush, New York) Begins
1972, quarterly. The basic indexing and
abstracting source for research in the study of
women.

1606. Women's Action Alliance. Women's Action
Almanac: A Complete Resource Guide, Williamson,
Jane; Diane Winston; and Wanda Wooten, eds. (New
York: William Morrow & Co., 1979)

1607. Women's Rights Law Reporter is a bimonthly
publication intended to cover areas of law which
especially affect women as women. Vol. 1- ;
1972- (New York)

1608. Women's Studies: An Interdisciplinary Journal.
Begins in 1973. A forum for the presentation
for scholarship and criticism about women in
many fields

1609. Women's Studies International Quarterly. Begins
in 1978, continues in 1982 as the Women's
Studies International Forum. A multidisciplin-
ary journal for the rapid publication of
research communications and review articles in
women's studies

1610. Women's Studies Quarterly. Begins spring 1972.
A publication of the Feminist Press and the
newsletter of the National Women's Studies
Association

1611. World Who's Who of Women, 1980. Kay, Ernest,
ed. 1980 (Cambridge, England: International
Biographical Center, Vol. 1 1973, updated
approximately every two years)

AUTHOR INDEX

Abbott, Sidney. 1
Abramson, Joan. 790, 1091
Acosta-Belen, Edna. 2
Adams, Carolyn Teich. 1092
Adams, Edith L. 1475
Adell, Judith. 509
Adelman, I. 583; see Bergman, B. R.
Agassi, Judith Buber. 566
Agonito, Rosemary. 1259
Aiken, William. 393
Albatross. 1476
Aldous, Joan. 1477
Alexander, Ralph A. 575; see Baas, Bernard M.
Allen, Christine Garside. 1260
Allen, Martha Leslie. 1478
Allen, Walters R. 4
Allen, W. R. 510
Almquist, Elizabeth McTaggart. 5, 567, 924
Altback, Edith Hosino. 6
Altman, Dennis. 7
American Archivist. 1577
American Jewish Archives and KTAV Publishing House. 1479
Amsden, Alice. 568
Amundsen, Kirsten. 8, 9, 867, 868
Andersen, Kristi. 869
Anderson, Karen. 204
Anderson, W. F. 29; see Brown, D. R.
Andre, Rae. 569
Annas, Julia. 1261, 1262

Cantor, Milton. 33, 600
Caplan, Arthur L. 323
Caraway, Hattie Wyatt. 984
Carden, Maren Lockwood. 34, 220
Carliner, G. 601
Carnegie Commission on Higher Education. 796
Carpenter, G. Russell. 344; see Gove, Walter
Carr, Timothy J. 457, 703; see Mott, Frank L.
Carroll, Bernice A. 35
Cassell, Joan. 36, 221
Cates, W. 1112
Cates, Willard, Jr. 409, 1113
Cayer, N. J. 985
Cech, Barbara. 1114
Center for the American Woman and Politics, Eagleton
    Institute. 1492
Ceulemans, Miek. 1493
Chaddock, Paul. 1145
Chafe, William H. 37, 222, 223, 928
Chafetz, Janet Saltzman. 324, 516, 986
Chamberlain, Hope. 987
Chandler, Melinda P. 1116
Chapman, J. Brad. 741; see Shaffer, Butler D.
Chapman, Jane Robert. 410
Chapman, R. 1412; see Pennock, J. H.
Chapman, Richard Allen. 1289
Chartered Life Underwriters Journal. 1196
Chenoweth, Lillian. 602
Chernow, Ron. 603
Cherry, Frances. 325
Chicana Research and Learning Center. 1538
Chilman, Catherine. 1117
Chisholm, Shirley. 39
Chiswick, Barry R. 604
Chodorow, Nancy. 326, 327, 328, 411, 1290
Chrissinger, M. S. 929
Christensen, Elia Hidalgo. 2; see Acosta-Belen, Edna
Christie, Claudia M. 930, 1118
Churgin, Jonah. 797
Clark, Albert P. 989
Clark, J. L. 517
Clark, Lorenne. 1291, 1292, 1293
Clarke, Harold D. 990

Lipsky, Michael. 949
Lloyd, Cynthia B. 685, 686; see also Niemi, Beth T.
  707
Locke, John. 1379
Loewy, Arnold H. 1173
Longavex y Vasquez, Enrigueta. 278
Lopata, Helena Znaniecki. 451, 687
Lott, Bernice. 361
Lougee, Carolyn C. 828
Loury, Glen C. 688
Love, Barbara. 1; see Abbott, Sidney
Lowe, Marian. 353, 362; see Hubbard, Ruth
Lowry, Helen. 624; see Ferber, Marianne
Luksetich, William A. 689
Lunardini, C. A. 279
Lydon, S. 363
Lyle, Jerolyn R. 690
Lynn, Naomi B. 898, 899, 1544; see also Flora,
  Cornelia B. 522; and Vaden, Richard E. 1077
McCarthy, John D. 128
McClain, E. 129
McCormack, Thelma. 1385
McCourt, Kathleen. 901, 1041
McCurdy, Jack. 829
McGrath, Michael C. Gargas. 1386
McGrath, Wilma E. 1042; see also Soule, John W. 911
McKee, Kathleen Burke. 1545
McMahon, Walter W. 806; see Ferber, Marianne A.
McPhee, Carol. 1546
McWilliams, Nancy. 130
Maccoby, Eleanor E. 364
MacDonald, M. 452
Mack, Delores E. 453
MacKenzie, Kyle. 59; see Elsasser, Nan
MacKinnon, Catherine A. 691
MacLeod, Jennifer S. 830
MacLeod, M. W. 1108; see Burstein, P.
MacManus, S. A. 1043
Mahoney, E. R. 692
Mahowald, Mary Briody. 1380
Malkiel, Burton G. 693, 1174
Malkiel, Judith A. 693, 1179; see Milkiel, Burton G.
Mandel, Ruth B. 1044; see also Fadely, Nancie. 1004

SUBJECT INDEX

Abortion, 150, 409, 1136, 1255; access to, 966, 1164,
    1171, 1202; attitudes toward, 1122; legal status
    of, 1113; opposition to, 464; public funding, 1122,
    1202; public policy, 1110, 1138
Academics, 790, 792, 797, 805, 814, 820, 845, 1064,
    1214
Achievement, 367, 612, 648, 813, 819, 979; attitudes
    toward, 325, 367, 511, 512, 539, 540, 556, 564,
    578, 634, 816, 835, 836, 838, 840, 1057;
    bibliography, 1502; educational, 808, 816, 831,
    833, 835
Activists, 896, 1061
Adams, Abigail, 312
Administrators, attitudes of, 1077; bibliography,
    1584, educational, 832. See also Management
Advisory commissions, 180, 192, 914, 918, 919, 1071,
    1109
AFDC, 477, 939, 947, 1156, 1170; clients 925, 955,
    971. See also Public assistance
Affirmative Action, 215, 597, 608, 683, 725, 728, 741,
    745, 753, 771, 789, 820, 826, 1121, 1140, 1143,
    1150, 1167, 1191, 1214, 1247, 1257, 1258;
    bibliography, 1585; enforcement of, 779. See also
    Job discrimination
Aged, 963, 975
Aging, 111, 1175; cultural construction of, 12
Air Force Academy, 854
Alcoholics, 1183
Alienation, 1137
Almanac, women's action, 1606; women's rights, 1511

Bakke case, 1140, 1143
Beliefs. See Attitude change; Attitude formation;
   Political attitudes; Political socialization;
   Socialization
Bentham, Jeremy, 1467
Bibliography of women's bibliographies, 1483, 1499
Biocultural approaches to evolution, 352
Biocultural approaches to gender, 316, 318, 322, 324,
   326, 332, 343, 344, 346, 349, 353, 357, 358, 359,
   370, 379, 382, 385, 1353
Biographical dictionaires 1522, 1525, 1551, 1552
Biological approaches to gender, 338, 341, 376, 1305
Biology, 343, 346, 348, 350, 359, 376, 378, 385, 390,
   391; history of, 812
Birth, 470
Birth control, 81, 90, 98. See also Contraception;
   Family planning
Black history, 275, 287; documents, 1541
Black lesbianism, bibliography, 1565
Black men, 481
Black power, 197
Black women, 3, 4, 5, 22, 29, 30, 47, 48, 52, 102,
   110, 123, 154, 156, 162, 169, 196, 218, 331, 409,
   480, 542, 580, 590, 603, 620, 682, 775, 832, 875,
   907, 932, 1113; bibliography, 1531, 1567, 1572,
   1573, 1601; documents, 1541; leaders, 995; status
   of, 924
Blacks, 23, 26, 154, 194, 197, 253, 304, 322, 407,
   416, 467, 501, 514, 588, 591, 644, 772, 894, 942,
   1154, 1183
Boards of directors, 1090
Bolshevism, 1326
Bureaucracy, 944, 949, 1055, 1056. See also
   Organizations, formal; Public administration
Bureaucrats, 1024. See also Leadership
Burger, Warren, Chief Justice, 1147
Business, 795, 1028, 1063, 1090
Businesses, women-owned, 763

California, 1109
Capitalism, 72, 283, 421, 438, 508, 616, 656, 694,
   701, 1298, 1311, 1358, 1362, 1453
Caraway, Hattie, 984

Curriculum, 822, 827, 828, 1512

Daley, Richard, 1060
Daughters, 554
Daycare. See Child care
Democracy, 867, 868. See also Political theory
Democratic National Convention (1972), 1042
Demography, 174, 455, 461, 666, 860. See also
    Population change
Dependency, 956, 957, 962
Dialectics, 52, 67, 331, 478, 749, 1328, 1331
Dictionaries, biographical, 1522, 1525, 1551, 1552
Directories, 1598, 1611
Discrimination, 15, 49, 115, 147, 179, 184, 187, 250,
    343, 348, 384, 617, 711, 793, 795, 824, 825, 826,
    846, 847, 924, 926, 927, 1035, 1091, 1124, 1128,
    1204, 1248, 1348; economic, 610; educational, 857.
    See also Job discrimination; Inequality
Division of labor, 283, 284, 395, 396, 414, 418, 419,
    436, 437, 440, 446, 449, 457, 458, 459, 460, 465,
    472, 477, 478, 492, 495, 498, 500, 502, 508, 533,
    543, 560, 568, 569, 573, 576, 582, 583, 586, 587,
    589, 593, 594, 595, 598, 609, 611, 615, 623, 635,
    639, 646, 656, 659, 660, 661, 663, 671, 677, 680,
    681, 684, 685, 694, 695, 697, 699, 702, 703, 705,
    709, 710, 716, 736, 737, 740, 742, 749, 759, 930,
    1182, 1186, 1250, 1344, 1453
Divorce, 1205, 1207
Divorcees, 441
Domestic labor, 72, 421, 434, 437, 438, 440, 459, 478,
    488, 502, 569, 603, 642, 661, 687, 702, 709, 710,
    754, 773, 1207, 1250, 1298, 1344, 1388, 1453
Domestic violence, 1231, 1232. See also Sexual
    violence; Violence
Douglass, Frederick, 232
Draft registration, 1224, 1254
Drug addiction, 950, 1114, 1183
Dual career couples, 533, 586, 695, 719, 720, 1187;
    bibliography, 1484
Dualism, 1347

501, 510, 513, 514, 528, 542, 545, 588, 601, 604,
605, 620, 626, 644, 682, 700, 750, 821, 860, 875,
881, 892, 924, 932, 942, 1154, 1354; bibliography,
1532
Euripides, 1442
European history, bibliography, 1508
Evolution, 332, 352, 358, 382
Executives, 1040. See also Leaders; Leadership
Existentialism, 1295, 1318

Family, 203, 204, 355, 381, 394, 395, 399, 408, 412,
415, 416, 418, 432, 453, 455, 472, 475, 496, 576,
664, 665, 975, 1104; bibliography, 1477, 1568;
black, 416, 417, 430, 479, 480, 510, 513, 591, 682,
1217; black, bibliography, 1531; effects of poverty
on, 425; extended, 451; female-headed, 441, 469,
503, 964, 1104, 1170, 1201, 1242; Greek, 1456;
history of, 302, 474, 486, 492; images of, 494;
native American, 431; nuclear, 448; origins of,
342, 428; power in the, 437, 488, 490; suburban,
454; theories of, 1289, 1313, 1317, 1323, 1337,
1387, 1442, 1448, 1449, 1460, 1462; white, 591
Family planning, 462, 961, 1110, 1136, 1171. See also
Birth control; Contraception
Family policy, 399, 443, 444, 450, 452, 483, 636, 671,
1094, 1095, 1117, 1133, 1141, 1144, 1161, 1163,
1166, 1178, 1192, 1206, 1219
Family structure, 327, 396, 397, 400, 407, 414, 418,
420, 424, 427, 434, 436, 438, 446, 447, 448, 450,
453, 458, 460, 461, 466, 476, 484, 485, 487, 490,
491, 498, 503, 506, 508, 532, 536, 585, 609, 611,
654, 656, 659, 671, 681, 684, 699, 703, 749, 943,
1026, 1094, 1096, 1177, 1187, 1205
Farms, 757
Fear of success, 835, 836, 838, 840. See also
Achievement, attitudes towards
Federal employment programs, 762
Federal executives, 1040
Federal government, 250, 762, 885, 1007, 1045, 1238
Female-headed families, 441, 469, 503, 731, 964, 1104,
1170, 1201, 1242
Femininity, 317, 319, 324, 327, 420, 535, 1322, 1337,
1342, 1357, 1438